The Pomeranian may be small, but don't let his size fool you! The Pom is actually descended from some of the heartiest dogs around: the sled dogs of Iceland and Lapland.

Poms weren't always toy dogs. Originally, they weighed anywhere from 20 to 30 pounds. It wasn't until they ended up in a German province called Pomerania that these companion dogs were bred down to their current size of 3 to 7 pounds.

Pomeranians were popularized in nineteenth century England by Queen Victoria, who loved her Poms so much she requested that her favorite one, Turi, be put in her bed to comfort her when she became ill. She died with her Pom beside her.

The Pomeranian is a lively dog and is bold and inquisitive, too. He usually mistakes himself for a big dog, fiercely and fearlessly protecting his family from any "invaders." The Pom makes an excellent watchdog.

Surprisingly, when it comes to grooming, the Pom's double coat only requires twice-weekly brushing, with an occasional scissors trim.

The Pomeranian gets enough exercise just from normal household living. However, he needs fresh air and sunshine, so give him a daily romp on the lawn.

Pomeranians come in an array of colors including red, black, blue, cream, choco-late, white, beaver, black and tan, and black and sable.

Featuring Photographs by
WINTER CHURCHILL PHOTOGRAPHY

Howell Book House
Published by Wiley Publishing, Inc. All rights reserved
Published simultaneously in Canada

For general information about our other products and services, please contact our Customer Care Department within the United States at (800) 762-2974, outside the United States at (317) 572-3993 or fax (317) 572-4002.

Wiley also publishes its books in a variety of electronic formats. Some content that appears in print may not be available in electronic books. For more information about Wiley products, visit our web site at www.wiley.com.

The Essential Pomeranian is an abridged edition of *The Pomeranian: An Owner's Guide to a Happy Healthy Pet,* first published in 1996.

Library of Congress Cataloging-in-Publication Data
     The essential pomeranian / featuring photographs by Winter Churchill Photography.
    p. cm.
    Includes bibliographical references (p.86-89) and index.
    ISBN 1-58245-074-9
    1. Pomeranian dog.
    SF429.P8E77 1999   99-12404
    636.76—dc21   CIP
Manufactured in the United States of America
10 9 8 7 6

Series Director: Michele Matrisciani
Production Team: Tammy Ahrens, Carrie Allen, AB Conder and Heather Pope
Book Design: Paul Costello

ARE YOU READY?!

☐ Have you prepared your home and your family for your new pet?

☐ Have you gotten the proper supplies you'll need to care for your dog?

☐ Have you found a veterinarian that you (and your dog) are comfortable with?

☐ Have you thought about how you want your dog to behave?

☐ Have you arranged your schedule to accommodate your dog's needs for exercise and attention?

No matter what stage you're at with your dog—still thinking about getting one, or he's already part of the family—this Essential guide will provide you with the practical information you need to understand and care for your canine companion. Of course you're ready—you have this book!

Pomeranian

SIGHT

Pomeranians can detect movement at a greater distance than we can, but they can't see as well up close. They can also see better in less light, but can't distinguish many colors.

SOUND

Poms, like all dogs, can hear about four times better than we can, and they can hear high-pitched sounds especially well.

TASTE

Pomeranians have fewer taste buds than we do, so they're likelier to try anything—and usually do, which is why it's important for their owners to monitor their food intake. Dogs are omnivorous, which means they eat meat as well as vegetables.

TOUCH

Poms are social animals and love to be petted, groomed and played with.

SMELL

A Pomeranian's nose is his greatest sensory organ. A dog's sense of smell is so great he can follow a trail that's weeks old, detect odors diluted to one-millionth the concentration we'd need to notice them, even sniff out a person under water!

CHAPTER ONE

Getting to Know Your Pomeranian

To live with a Pomeranian is to live with a dog of contrasts. He gives love, affection and loyalty in a deferential manner, yet at the same time radiates demanding arrogance. His body is small, his bones fragile, yet, if challenged, he will take on a Rottweiler. A happy-go-lucky lapdog, the playboy of the dog world, he will leave his privileged life to serve the deaf, herd ducks, track or work in obedience.

He stands all of five pounds and thinks he's fifty-five. Breeders

The Pomeranian excels in obedience.

Pomeranians are dedicated and loving companions.

may have made the Pom's body smaller but they didn't reduce his self-image, and today's Pom thinks he's still a large dog. The Pom is a little ball of fluff with a big personality and fulfills his owner's needs by being the perfect companion.

He starts out by living a long life, around fourteen to seventeen years, which means he offers more years of love and companionship than another breed of a larger variety. The Pom also gives lots of love to his family. Jumping around like a bouncing ball, he will greet you with ecstasy. He will lay next to you on the couch or at your feet in quiet fellowship or cuddle on your lap. Wherever you go in the house you will hear the little pit-pat of his feet as he follows you from room to room. After all, how can he take care of his loved ones when he's not with them?

A LOYAL AND PROTECTIVE LITTLE KING

All good kings protect their subjects, and the Pomeranian takes this responsibility very seriously. The least sign of intrusion, the smallest sound, a hint of invasion

CHARACTERISTICS OF THE POMERANIAN

protective	delicate
energetic	confident
affectionate	loyal
mischievous	

from someone outside your home, will bring on a burst of furious indignation. When the imagined threat is over, he puffs out his chest, struts about, clearly put out that someone would have the nerve to approach his territory. Of course, if

3

The little Pom has a strong will to protect and will not back down to any threats in order to keep his family safe.

The Pomeranian is an entertaining little character, and his quixotic actions will give you many hours of entertainment.

the intruder turns out to be a visitor, his royal manners appear and he issues lots of kisses and wags to the guest. His hearing is so acute that you will never need an alarm system. If you have a larger dog in your household, you will find that your Pom will hear sounds long before the other dog.

He's Not Always Royal

Your little king doesn't always act like a paragon of virtue, especially when young. You need to remember that a little prince or princess can get into trouble. Keep a close eye on

your little Pom while he is young and enroll him in puppy classes. The extra training and socialization will enable you to raise a very well-mannered pet.

AN ECLECTIC PET

Take notice that the Pomeranian's working background will occasionally pop up. More than one member of the American Pomeranian Club (APC) have reported that they own a Pom who loves to herd ducks or chickens. Using appropriately sized sleds, teams of Pomeranians in the late 1980s proved that they still can do the job when they demonstrated sled-pulling at APC Specialty shows.

There are Poms who love to do serious work. The best example is hearing-assistance dogs, another is tracking. Yep, you read it right— tracking. Our pampered lapdog with the royal attitude will leave his soft couch and warm hearth for the outdoor life.

The Pomeranian will often display a loving sensitivity toward his fellow creatures and use his smarts to solve problems that arise in his dog world.

A FRAGILE LITTLE FELLOW

Parents must take great care to teach their young children to be gentle and considerate *before* even thinking of aquiring a Pom. As with any breed, Poms make great companions for children, if the children have been properly prepared for a pet. Because he has a petite structure and tends to resemble a stuffed toy, the Pomeranian has no defense against the energy of a very young child.

protect the Pom if you also own a larger dog. When dogs are properly socialized, they get along and do not harm each other, regardless of the breed. However, if you own a dog that has harmed another in a fight, the two should never be left alone together. This is especially important when there is a great disparity in size. Never leave them alone unsupervised.

INTELLIGENT AND SOCIABLE

Pomeranians get along well with other animals in the household, though you have to be careful to

CHAPTER TWO

Homecoming

Before bringing home your new family member, do a little planning to help make the transition easier. The first decision to make is where the puppy will live. Will she have access to the entire house or be limited to certain rooms? A similar consideration applies to the yard. It is simpler to control a puppy's activities and to housetrain the puppy if she is confined to definite areas. If doors do not exist where needed, baby gates make satisfactory temporary barriers.

A dog crate is an excellent investment and is an invaluable aid in raising a puppy. It provides a safe, quiet place where a dog can sleep. If it's used properly, a crate helps with housetraining. However, long periods of uninterrupted stays are not recommended—especially for young puppies. If ever a puppy soils her crate because she has been confined for too long, she will be really difficult to housebreak. Unless you have someone at home or can have someone come in a few times a day to let her out to relieve herself and socialize with her for a while, a small crate is not advisable. Never lock a young puppy in a small crate for more than one hour!

Make sure your Pomeranian will have company and companionship during the day. If the members of your family are not at home during the day, try to come home at lunchtime, let your puppy out and spend some time with her. If this isn't possible, try to get a neighbor or friend who lives close by to come spend time with the puppy. Your Pomeranian thrives on human attention and guidance, and a puppy left alone most of the day will find ways to get your attention, most of them not so cute and many downright destructive.

ACCESSORIES

The breeder should tell you what your puppy has been eating. Buy some of this food and have it on hand when your puppy arrives. Keep the puppy on the food and feeding schedule of the breeder, especially for the first few days. If you want to switch foods after that, introduce the new one slowly, gradually adding

more and more to the old until it has been entirely replaced.

Your puppy will need a close-fitting nylon or cotton-webbed collar. This collar should be adjustable so that it can be used for the first couple of months. A properly fit collar is tight enough that it will not slip over the head, yet an adult finger fits easily under it. A puppy should never wear a choke chain or any other adult training collar.

In addition to a collar, you'll need a 4-to-6-foot-long leash. One made of nylon or cotton-webbed material is a fine and inexpensive first leash. It does not need to be more than $1/2$ inch in width. It is important to make sure that the clip

A baby gate is a great tool to keep your Pomeranian confined to areas of the house that are safe for her.

7

Chew toys are an excellent diversion for a teething puppy.

Protect your Pom by having her wear a collar and an ID tag with your name and phone number on it.

with your Pomeranian would be appropriate. Get a somewhat larger size than you immediately need to allow for growth.

Excessive chewing can be partially resolved by providing a puppy with her own chew toys. Small-size dog biscuits are good for the teeth and also act as an amusing toy. Do not buy chew toys composed of compressed particles, as these particles disintegrate when chewed and can get stuck in the puppy's throat. Hard rubber toys are also good for chewing, as are large rawhide bones. Avoid the smaller chewsticks, as they can splinter and choke the puppy. Anything given to a dog must be large enough that it cannot be swallowed.

The final starter items a puppy will need are a water bowl and food dish. You can select a smaller food

is of excellent quality and cannot become unclasped on its own. You will need one or two leads for walking the dog, as well as a collar or harness. If you live in a cold climate, a sweater or jacket for excursions dish for your puppy and then get a bigger one when your dog matures. Bowls are available in plastic, stainless steel and even ceramic. Stainless steel is probably the best choice, as it is practically indestructible. Non-spill dishes are available for the dog that likes to play in her water.

Identification

You will have to provide your puppy with some means of identification.

The first option is a common identification tag attached to the puppy's collar, bearing your name and phone number. This is the first thing someone who finds your Pomeranian will look for, and the information on it is straightforward and accessible. However, puppies can easily slip out of collars, and tags can fall off, so it is important to have a more permanent method of identification as well.

A microchip can also be used to identify your dog. A veterinarian can inject a tiny microchip encoded with your Pomeranian's information under her skin. Many animal shelters and vet's offices have the scanner to read the chip, and it cannot get lost or be removed. However, until the scanners (expensive pieces

PUPPY ESSENTIALS

To prepare yourself and your family for your puppy's homecoming, and to be sure your pup has what she needs, you should obtain the following:

Food and Water Bowls: One for each. We recommend stainless steel or heavy crockery—something solid but easy to clean.

Bed and/or Crate Pad: Something soft, washable and big enough for your soon-to-be-adult dog.

Crate: Make housetraining easier and provide a safe, secure den for your dog with a crate—it only looks like a cage to you!

Toys: As much fun to buy as they are for your pup to play with. Don't overwhelm your puppy with too many toys, though, especially the first few days she's home. And be sure to include something hollow you can stuff with goodies, like a Kong.

I.D. Tag: Inscribed with your name and phone number.

Collar: An adjustable buckle collar is best. Remember, your pup's going to grow fast!

Leash: Style is nice, but durability and your comfort while holding it count, too. You can't go wrong with leather for most dogs.

Grooming Supplies: The proper brushes, special shampoo, toenail clippers, a toothbrush and doggy toothpaste.

HOUSEHOLD DANGERS

Curious puppies and inquisitive dogs get into trouble not because they are bad, but simply because they want to investigate the world around them. It's our job to protect our dogs from harmful substances, like the following:

In the Garage

antifreeze

garden supplies, like snail and slug bait, pesticides, fertilizers, mouse and rat poisons

In the House

cleaners, especially pine oil

perfumes, colognes, aftershaves

medications, vitamins

office and craft supplies

electric cords

chicken or turkey bones

chocolate, onions

some house and garden plants, like ivy, oleander and poinsettia

of equipment) are more widely available, it is preferable to choose another form of identification as well.

The third method is a tattoo of some identifying number (your

Social Security number, your dog's AKC number) placed on the inside of your dog's hind leg. A tattoo is easily noticed and located, and it requires no sophisticated machinery to read. Anyone finding a lost dog with a tattoo will inform a vet or local animal shelter who will know what to do.

The single best preventive measure one can take is to housebreak and chewtoy train your Pom so that she may safely and comfortably spend her days indoors. If your Pom is to be an indoor/outdoor dog, then a completely fenced yard is a must. If you have a fence, it should be carefully inspected to insure there are no holes or gaps in it, and no places where a vigorous and mischievous puppy could escape by digging an escape path under the fence.

PUPPY-PROOFING

Outside

If you do not have a fenced yard, it would be useful to provide at least an outside kennel area where the puppy could safely relieve himself. Failing that, the youngster should be walked outdoors on a lead several times a day, taking care at first that

Providing your Pomeranian with a fenced-in yard is the best way to keep her from being lost or stolen.

the lead is sufficiently tight around her neck so that she cannot slip out of it.

Inside

You will also need to puppy-proof your home. Curious puppies will get into everything everywhere. Even if you generally keep your Pomeranian close to you or in her indoor or out-door enclosure, there will be times when she wants to explore and you cannot watch her. Make sure your home has been puppy-proofed so you can be reasonably confident she won't do serious damage to herself or your home.

Keep cabinets locked in order to protect your curious Pom from finding toxic household substances.

Securely stow away all household cleaners and other poisonous products such as antifreeze which, unfortunately, has a taste dogs seem to love. Keep all electrical cords out of reach, and secure electrical outlets.

Make sure you have removed poisonous plants from your house and garden. Puppies put everything into their mouths, and you need to make sure there's nothing dangerous they can get into. Inside, dangerous plants include poinsettia, ivy and philodendron. Outside, holly, hydrangea and azalea are among the plants of which your puppy should steer clear. The bulbs and root systems of daffodils, tulips and others are also poisonous.

THE ALL-IMPORTANT ROUTINE

Most puppies do best if their lives follow a schedule. They need definite and regular periods of time for playing, eating and sleeping. Puppies like to start their day early. This is a good time to take a walk or play some games of fetch. After breakfast, most are ready for a nap. How often this pattern is repeated will depend on one's daily routine. Sometimes it is easier for a working person or family to stick with a regular schedule than it is for someone who is home all of the time.

Most dogs reach their peaks of activity and need the least amount of rest from 6 months to 3 years of age. As they mature, they spend increasingly longer periods of time sleeping. It is important to make an effort to ensure that a Pomeranian receives sufficient exercise each day to keep her in proper weight and fitness throughout her life. Puppies need short periods of exercise, but, due to the fact that their bodies are developing, should never be exercised to excess. Walking is more suitable for Pomeranians than running.

CHAPTER THREE

To Good Health

FIRST THINGS FIRST

By and large, Pomeranians are a healthy and hardy little breed—usually living to a ripe old age. They are, however, more susceptible to one or two diseases and conditions.

Anesthesia

Like other toy breeds, the Pomeranian doesn't tolerate anesthesia very well, especially when more than one procedure is performed. Isoflourane, a relatively new anesthetic, works safely on the Pom, and most veterinarians are now using it. Most deaths of Pomeranians while under anesthesia seem to happen when the vet performs lengthy procedures or two procedures at the same time, such as spaying and teeth cleaning.

Pomeranians are the quintessential companion dog.

Black Skin and Baldness

Several health problems, such as Cushing's disease, hypothyroidism, cortisone excess and estrogen deficiency cause bald areas of dark gray skin. But in the Pomeranian breed, the most common cause of these symptoms is what the Pomeranian fancier calls "black skin disease." Some also call it elephant skin disease, the Pom disease or simply the skin disease.

Veterinarians diagnose it as adult growth hormone disorder. Before buying a Pomeranian ask the breeder if any of the puppies' ancestors had the black skin disease. Or even better, make sure you get to meet as many of your prospective puppy's relatives as possible—check that they are *all* healthy and well behaved! Lack of hair would be very obvious. Also ask if any older puppies from the sire and dam of your prospective pup have come down with this condition.

Signs of black skin disease do not appear right away. At 6 months, Pomeranian puppies start growing their adult coat. With black skin disease, the puppy retains the juvenile coat and he never gets an adult coat. At about 18 months old, the puppy coat starts falling out and he goes bald. In some cases, the puppy will get the adult coat and go bald later. These Poms usually do not lose as much hair as the ones who never grew adult fur.

As the dog develops bald patches, his skin turns a dark gray color. It may remain smooth or get a little rough, but it doesn't develop any open sores or an offensive odor. The condition appears more often in males. The tail, rump and backs of thighs go bald. Some dogs lose all their belly hair and others go completely bald except for the legs and head. Otherwise, the dog remains healthy.

No cure for this condition exists, but sometimes the coat can be made to grow again. Often, neutering the male brings back the coat, but this doesn't work for every Pom. To further confuse the issue, the coat sometimes comes back when the Pom reaches 7 years old. Hormone replacement shots can induce coat growth, but they are expensive and may cause the dog to develop diabetes. If you suspect your Pom may have this disease, consult your veterinarian.

Hypoglycemia

This sudden drop in blood sugar occurs more often in the toy breeds. It usually happens to very young puppies, but in severely stressful situations it also can affect an adult Pomeranian. Heavy activity, the stress of a new home, stomach upsets, head injuries and severe pain can cause the condition.

The symptoms entail sudden collapse, weakness, tremors and sometimes convulsions. If left untreated it can lead to coma and death.

For prevention in an adult Pomeranian, feed a good-quality dog food with a low glycemic index.

15

Regular visits to the veterinarian will help you monitor your Pomeranian's health.

Preventive care means proactively preventing diseases, like feeding your Pom properly to avoid hypoglycemia.

Feeding your Pom twice a day or two or three small meals a day can increase the digestibility of the food, which will help keep blood sugar in check. Make sure your Pom's food maintains a proper protein/carbohydrate balance. Feed meals consisting of complex carbohydrates only, which release glucose at a steady rate. Do not feed your Pom simple sugars, such as corn syrup. Anytime a dog becomes unconscious, call your veterinarian.

Hypothyroidism

Loss of hair from the dog's back and thighs, along with sluggishness,

weight gain, scaling skin and intolerance to cold indicates hypothyroidism, though sometimes a distinct change in personality is the only symptom. Your veterinarian can diagnose this treatable condition with a blood test.

Patellar Luxation

A condition in which the kneecap slips out of its groove, luxation is common in the toy breeds. It is usually an inherited disorder but also can be caused by an injury. The degree of luxation varies from a mild case that barely affects the dog to a severe one that requires surgery.

Don't let a diagnosis of patellar luxation discourage you. The majority of Pomeranians with this condition live normal lives, and if your puppy's luxation is severe, surgery will take care of the problem.

THE IMPORTANCE OF PREVENTIVE CARE

There are many aspects of preventive care with which Pomeranian owners should be familiar: A good diet, vaccinations, regular vet visits and tooth care are just some.

16

The earlier that illness is detected in the Pomeranian, the easier it is for the veterinarian to treat the problem. Owners can help ensure their dogs' health by being on the lookout for medical problems. All this requires is an eye for detail and a willingness to observe. Pay close attention to your Pomeranian, how he looks, how he acts. What is normal behavior? How does his coat usually look? What are his eating and sleeping patterns? Subtle changes can indicate a problem. Keep close tabs on what is normal for your Pomeranian, and if anything out of the ordinary develops, call the veterinarian.

Spaying and Neutering

Spaying or neutering—surgically altering the Pomeranian so she or he cannot reproduce—should be at the top of every owner's "To Do" list. Why?

First, every day thousands of puppies are born in the United States as a result of uncontrolled breeding. For every pet living in a happy home today, there are four pets on the street or in abusive homes suffering from starvation, exposure, neglect or mistreatment.

ADVANTAGES OF SPAY/NEUTER

The greatest advantage of spaying (for females) or neutering (for males) your dog is that you are guaranteed that your dog will not produce puppies. There are too many puppies already available for too few homes. There are other advantages as well.

Advantages of Spaying

No messy heats.

No "suitors" howling at your windows or waiting in your yard.

No risk of pyometra (disease of the uterus) and decreased incidences of mammary cancer.

Advantages of Neutering

Decreased incidences of fighting, but does not affect the dog's personality.

Decreased roaming in search of bitches in season.

Decreased incidences of many urogenital diseases.

In six years, a single female dog and her offspring can be the source of 67,000 new dogs.

A second reason to spay or neuter your Pomeranian is to create a healthier, more well-adjusted pet that, in most cases, will live longer than an intact animal. A spayed

17

female is no longer susceptible to pyometra (infection of uterus), and is less prone to mammary cancers. The procedure eliminates the behavior that accompanies the female's heat cycle. A neutered male is less likely to develop prostate or anal cancer and is less apt to roam. Marking behavior is also reduced by altering and your dog will not be picked on as much by other male dogs!

When should your Pomeranian be spayed or neutered? Recommendations vary among vets, but 6 months of age is commonly suggested. Ask your vet what age is best for your Pomeranian.

Vaccinations

Another priority on a Pomeranian owner's list of preventive care is vaccinations. Vaccinations protect the dog against a host of infectious diseases, preventing illnesses and the misery that accompanies them.

Vaccines should be a part of every young puppy's health care, since youngsters are so susceptible to disease. To remain effective, vaccinations must be kept current.

Good Nutrition

Dogs that receive the appropriate nutrients daily will be healthier and stronger than those that do not. The

These little guys are happy and healthy thanks to vaccines.

proper balance of proteins, fats, carbohydrates, vitamins, minerals and sufficient water enables the dog to remain healthy by fighting off illness and is essential for Poms to help prevent hypoglycemia.

Routine Checkups

Regular visits to the veterinary clinic should begin when your Pomeranian is a young pup and continue throughout his life. Make this a habit and it will certainly contribute to your Pomeranian's good health. Even if your Pomeranian seems perfectly healthy, a checkup once or twice a year is in order. Even if your dog seems fine to you, he could have an ongoing problem. Your veterinarian is trained to notice subtle changes or hints of illness.

Well-Being

Aside from the dog's physical needs—a proper and safe shelter, nutritious diet, health care and regular exercise—the Pomeranian needs plenty of plain, old-fashioned love. The dog is happiest when he is part of a family, enjoying the social interactions, nurturing and play. Bringing the Pomeranian into the family provides him with a sense of security.

PREVENTIVE CARE PAYS

Using common sense, paying attention to your dog and working with your veterinarian, you can minimize health risks and problems. Use vet-recommended flea, tick and heartworm preventive medications; feed a nutritious diet appropriate for your dog's size, age and activity level; give your dog sufficient exercise and regular grooming; train and socialize your dog; keep current on your dog's shots; and enjoy all the years you have with your friend.

COMMON DISEASES

Rabies

Rabies is preventable with routine vaccines, and such vaccinations are required by law for domestic animals in all states in this country.

Probably one of the most well-known diseases that can affect dogs, rabies can strike any warm-blooded animal (including humans)—and is fatal. The rabies virus, which is present in an affected animal's saliva, is usually spread through a bite or open wound. The signs of the disease can be subtle at first. Normally friendly pets can become irritable and withdrawn. Shy pets may become overly friendly. Eventually,

19

FLEAS AND TICKS

There are so many safe, effective products available now to combat fleas and ticks that—thankfully—they are less of a problem. Prevention is key, however. Ask your veterinarian about starting your puppy on a flea/tick repellant right away. With this, regular grooming and environmental controls, your dog and your home should stay pest-free. Without this attention, you risk infesting your dog and your home, and you're in for an ugly and costly battle to clear up the problem.

the dog becomes withdrawn and avoids light, which hurts the eyes of a rabid dog. Fever, vomiting and diarrhea are common.

Once these symptoms develop, the animal will die; there is no treatment or cure.

Since rabid animals may have a tendency to be aggressive and bite, animals suspected of having rabies should only be handled by animal control handlers or veterinarians.

Parvovirus

Canine Parvovirus is prevalent, but preventable with vaccinations. It is a highly contagious and devastating illness. The hardy virus is usually transmitted through contaminated feces, but it can be carried on an infected dog's feet or skin. It strikes dogs of all ages and is most serious in young puppies.

There are two main types of parvovirus. The first signs of the diarrhea-syndrome type are usually depression and lack of appetite, followed by vomiting and the characteristic bloody diarrhea. The dog appears to be in great pain, and he usually has a high fever.

The cardiac-syndrome type affects the heart muscle and is most common in young puppies. Puppies with this condition will stop nursing, whine and gasp for air. Death may occur suddenly or in a few days. Youngsters that recover can have lingering heart failure that eventually takes their life.

Veterinarians can treat dogs with parvovirus, but the outcome varies. It depends on the age of the animal and severity of the disease and how much money an owner is willing to spend. Treatment generally works, but it takes some time and is expensive, so vaccinate to prevent it. Treatment may include fluid therapy, medication to stop the severe diarrhea and antibiotics to prevent or stop secondary infection.

Young puppies receive antibody protection against the disease from their mother, but they lose it quickly and must be vaccinated to prevent the disease. In most cases, vaccinated puppies are protected against the disease.

Coronavirus

Vaccinations are available to protect puppies and dogs against the virus and are recommended especially for all puppies and those dogs in frequent contact with other dogs.

Canine coronavirus is especially devastating to young puppies, causing depression, lack of appetite, vomiting that may contain blood and characteristically yellow-orange diarrhea. The virus is transmitted through feces, urine and saliva, and the onset of symptoms is usually rapid.

Dogs suffering from coronavirus are treated similarly to those suffering from parvovirus: fluid therapy, medication to stop diarrhea and vomiting and antibiotics if necessary.

Distemper

Caused by a virus, distemper is highly contagious and is most com-

YOUR PUPPY'S VACCINES

Vaccines are given to prevent your dog from getting infectious diseases like canine distemper or rabies. Vaccines are the ultimate preventive medicine: They're given before your dog ever gets the disease so as to protect him from the disease. That's why it is necessary for your dog to be vaccinated routinely. Puppy vaccines start at 8 weeks of age for the five-in-one DHLPP vaccine and are given every three to four weeks until the puppy is 16 months old. Your veterinarian will put your puppy on a proper schedule and will remind you when to bring in your dog for shots.

mon in unvaccinated puppies aged 3 to 8 months, but older dogs are susceptible as well. Fortunately, due to modern-day vaccines, distemper is no longer the killer it was fifty years ago.

It is especially important to vaccinate bitches before breeding to ensure maternal antibodies in the pups.

Hepatitis

Hepatitis is preventable in dogs by keeping vaccinations current.

Infectious canine hepatitis can affect dogs of every age, but it is most severe in puppies. It primarily affects the dog's liver, kidneys and lining of the blood vessels. Highly contagious, it is transmitted through urine, feces and saliva.

This disease has several forms. In the fatal fulminating form, the dog becomes ill very suddenly, develops bloody diarrhea and dies. In the acute form, the dog develops a fever, has bloody diarrhea, vomits blood and refuses to eat. Jaundice may be present; the whites of the dog's eyes appear yellow. Dogs with a mild case are lethargic or depressed and often refuse to eat.

Infectious canine hepatitis must be diagnosed and confirmed with a blood test. Ill dogs require hospitalization.

Lyme Disease

Lyme disease has received a lot of press recently, with its increased incidence throughout the United States. The illness, caused by the bacteria *Borrelia burgdorferi*, is carried by ticks. It is passed along when the tick bites a victim, canine or human. (The dog cannot pass the disease to people, though. It is only transmitted via the tick.)

In dogs, the disease manifests itself in sudden lameness caused by swollen joints, similar to arthritis. The dog is weak and may run a fever. The lameness can last a few days or several months, and some dogs have recurring difficulties.

Antibiotics are very effective in treating Lyme disease, and the sooner it is diagnosed and treated, the better. A vaccine is available; ask your veterinarian if your dog would benefit from it.

Kennel Cough

"Kennel cough," or the more politically correct "canine cough," shows itself as a harsh, dry cough. This contagious disease has been termed "kennel cough" because of its often rapid spread through kennels. The cough may persist for weeks and is often followed by a bout of chronic bronchitis.

Many kennels require proof of bordatella vaccination before

Three types of ticks (l–r): the wood tick, brown dog tick and deer tick.

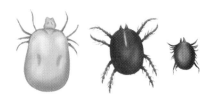

22

boarding. If your dog is in and out of kennels frequently, vaccination certainly is not a bad idea.

FIRST AID

First aid is not a substitute for professional care, though it can help save a dog's life.

To Stop Bleeding

Bleeding from a severe cut or wound must be stopped right away. There are two basic techniques—direct pressure and the tourniquet.

Try to control bleeding first by using direct pressure. Ask an assistant to hold the injured Pomeranian and place several pads of sterile gauze over the wound. Press. Do not wipe the wound or apply any cleansers or ointments. Apply firm, even pressure. If blood soaks through the pad, do not remove it as this could disrupt clotting. Simply place another pad on top and continue to apply pressure.

If bleeding on a leg or the tail does not stop by applying pressure, try using a tourniquet. Use this only as a last resort. A tourniquet that is left on too long can result in limb loss.

POISON ALERT

If your dog has ingested a potentially poisonous substance, waste no time. Call the National Animal Poison Control Center hot line:

(800) 548-2423 ($30 per case) or

(900) 680-0000 ($20 first five minutes; $2.95 each additional minute)

If the dog is bleeding from his mouth or rectum, or vomits or defecates blood, he may be suffering from internal injuries. Call the veterinarian right away for emergency treatment.

Shock

Whenever a dog is injured or is seriously ill, the odds are good that he will go into a state of shock. A decreased supply of oxygen to the tissues usually results in unconsciousness, pale gums, weak, rapid pulse and labored, rapid breathing. If not treated, a dog will die from shock. The conditions of the dog should continue to be treated, but the dog should be as comfortable as possible. A blanket can help keep a dog warm. A dog in shock needs immediate veterinary care.

23

It is important to know the first-aid basics—just in case your Pom gets into things he shouldn't.

24

- Call your veterinarian and follow his or her directions.

- Try to identify the poison source. This is really important. Take the container or plant to the clinic.

Heatstroke

Heatstroke can be deadly and must be treated immediately to save the dog. Signs include rapid panting, darker-than-usual gums and tongue, salivating, exhaustion or vomiting. The dog's body temperature is elevated, sometimes as high as 106°F. If the dog is not treated, coma and death can follow.

If heatstroke is suspected, cool down your overheated dog as quickly as possible by immersing him in cold water, and call your veterinarian. Mildly affected dogs can be moved to a cooler environment, into an air-conditioned home, for example, or wrapped in moistened towels.

Poisoning

A dog's curiosity will often lead him to eat or lick things he shouldn't. Unfortunately, many substances are poisonous to dogs, including household products, plants or chemicals. Owners must learn to act quickly if poisoning is suspected because the results can be deadly.

If your dog appears to be poisoned:

Insect Bites/Stings

Just like people, dogs can suffer bee stings and insect bites. Bees, wasps and yellow jackets leave a nasty, painful sting, and if your dog is stung repeatedly shock can occur.

If an insect bite is suspected, try to identify the culprit. Remove the stinger if it is a bee sting, and apply a mixture of baking soda and water to the sting. It is also a good idea to apply ice packs to reduce inflammation and ease pain. Call your veterinarian, especially if your dog seems ill or goes into shock.

INTERNAL PARASITES

Dogs are susceptible to several internal parasites. Keeping your Pomeranian free of internal parasites is another important aspect of health care.

Watch for general signs of poor condition: a dull coat, weight loss, lethargy, coughing, weakness and diarrhea.

For proper diagnosis and treatment of internal parasites, consult a veterinarian.

Roundworms

Roundworms, or ascarids, are probably the most common worms that affect dogs. Most puppies are born with these organisms in their intestines, which is why youngsters are treated for these parasites as soon as it is safe to do so.

Animals contract roundworms by ingesting infected soil and

25

Regular veterinary checkups, daily exercise, balanced nutrition and a lot of old-fashioned TLC will help keep your Pomeranian happy and healthy.

WHAT'S WRONG WITH MY DOG?

We've listed some common conditions of health problems and their possible causes. If any of the following conditions appear serious or persist for more than 24 hours, make an appointment to see your veterinarian immediately.

CONDITIONS	POSSIBLE CAUSES
DIARRHEA	Intestinal upset, typically caused by eating something bad or overeating. Can also be a viral infection, a bad case of nerves or anxiety or a parasite infection. If you see blood in the feces, get to the vet right away.
VOMITING/RETCHING	Dogs regurgitate fairly regularly (bitches for their young), whenever something upsets their stomach, or even out of excitement or anxiety. Often dogs eat grass, which, because it's indigestible in its pure form, irritates their stomachs and causes them to vomit. Getting a good look at *what* your dog vomited can better indicate what's causing it.
COUGHING	Obstruction in the throat; virus (kennel cough); roundworm infestation; congestive heart failure.
RUNNY NOSE	Because dogs don't catch colds like people, a runny nose is a sign of congestion or irritation.
LOSS OF APPETITE	Because most dogs are hearty and regular eaters, a loss of appetite can be your first and most accurate sign of a serious problem.
LOSS OF ENERGY (LETHARGY)	Any number of things could be slowing down your dog, from an infection to internal tumors to overexercise—even overeating.

feces, so clean it up immediately. A roundworm infestation can rob vital nutrients from young puppies and cause diarrhea, vomiting and digestive upset. Roundworms can also harm a young animal's liver and lungs, so treatment is imperative.

CONDITIONS	POSSIBLE CAUSES
STINKY BREATH	Imagine if you never brushed your teeth! Foul-smelling breath indicates plaque and tartar buildup that could possibly have caused infection. Start brushing your dog's teeth.
LIMPING	This could be caused by something as simple as a hurt or bruised pad, to something as complicated as hip dysplasia, torn ligaments or broken bones.
CONSTANT ITCHING	Probably due to fleas, mites or an allergic reaction to food or environment (your vet will need to help you determine what your dog's allergic to).
RED, INFLAMED, ITCHY SPOTS	Often referred to as "hot spots," these are particularly common on coated breeds. They're caused by a bacterial infection that gets aggravated as the dog licks and bites at the spot.
BALD SPOTS	These are the result of excessive itching or biting at the skin so that the hair follicles are damaged; excessively dry skin; mange; calluses; and even infections. You need to determine what the underlying cause is.
STINKY EARS/HEAD SHAKING	Take a look under your dog's ear flap. Do you see brown, waxy buildup? Clean the ears with something soft and a special cleaner, and don't use cotton swabs or go too deep into the ear canal.
UNUSUAL LUMPS	Could be fatty tissue, could be something serious (infection, trauma, tumor). Don't wait to find out.

27

Tapeworms

Tapeworms are commonly transmitted by fleas to dogs. Tapeworm eggs enter the body of a canine host when the animal accidentally ingests a carrier flea. The parasite settles in the intestines, where it sinks its head into the intestinal wall and feeds off

WHEN TO CALL THE VETERINARIAN

In any emergency situation, you should call your veterinarian immediately. Try to stay calm when you call, and give the vet or the assistant as much information as possible before you leave for the clinic. That way, the staff will be able to take immediate, specific action when you arrive. Emergencies include:

- Bleeding or deep wounds
- Hyperthermia (overheating)
- Shock
- Dehydration
- Abdominal Pain
- Burns
- Fits
- Unconsciousness
- Broken bones
- Paralysis

Call your veterinarian if you suspect any health troubles.

material the host is digesting. The worm grows a body of egg packets, which break off periodically and are expelled from the body in the feces.

Fleas then ingest the eggs from the feces and the parasite's life cycle begins all over again.

Hookworms

Hookworms are so named because they hook onto an animal's small intestine and suck the host's blood. Like roundworms, hookworms are contracted when a dog ingests contaminated soil or feces.

Hookworms can be especially devastating to dogs. They will become thin and sick; puppies can die. An affected dog will suffer from bloody diarrhea and, if the parasites migrate to the lungs, the dog may contract bronchitis or pneumonia.

Hookworms commonly strike puppies 2 to 8 weeks of age and are less common in adult dogs.

Whipworms

Known for their thread-like appearance, whipworms attach into the wall of the large intestine to feed. Thick-shelled eggs are passed in the feces and in about two to four weeks are mature and able to reinfect a host that ingests the eggs.

Mild whipworm infestation is often without signs, but as the worms grow, weight loss, bloody diarrhea and anemia follow. In areas where the soil is heavily contaminated, frequent checks are advised to prevent severe infestation.

Heartworms

Heartworm larvae are transmitted by the ordinary mosquito, but the effects are far from ordinary. In three to four months, the larvae (microfilaria) become small worms and make their way to a vein, where they are transported to the heart, where they grow and reproduce.

At first, a dog with heartworms is free of symptoms. The signs vary, but the most common is a deep cough and shortness of breath. The dog tires easily, is weak and loses weight. Eventually, the dog may suffer from congestive heart failure.

EXTERNAL PARASITES

FLEAS—Besides carrying tapeworm larvae, fleas bite and suck the host's blood. Their bites itch and are extremely annoying to dogs, especially if the dog is hypersensitive to the bite. Fleas must be eliminated on the dog with special shampoos and dips. Fleas also infest the dog's bedding and the owner's home and yard.

TICKS—Several varieties of ticks attach themselves to dogs, where they burrow into the skin and suck blood. Ticks can be carriers of several diseases, including Lyme disease and Rocky Mountain Spotted Fever.

Because your Pom will not spend a lot of time outdoors, he may be more susceptible to external parasites, intense heat and insect bites and stings.

LICE—Lice are not common in dogs, but when they are present they cause intense irritation and itching. There are two types: biting and sucking. Biting lice feed on skin scales, and sucking lice feed on blood.

MITES—There are several types of mites that cause several kinds of mange, including sarcoptic, demodectic and cheyletiella. These microscopic mites cause intense itching and misery to the dog.

CHAPTER FOUR

Positively Nutritious

The nutritional needs of a dog change throughout her lifetime. It is necessary to be aware of these changes not only for proper initial growth to occur, but also so your dog can lead a healthy life for many years.

Before bringing your puppy home, ask the breeder for the puppy's feeding schedule and information about what and how much she is used to eating. Maintain this regimen for at least the first few days before gradually changing to a schedule that is more in line with your family's lifestyle. The breeder may supply you with a small quantity of the food the puppy has been eating. Use this or have your own supply of the same food ready when you bring your puppy home.

Your Pomeranian's nutritional requirements will change throughout her lifetime.

After the puppy has been with you for three days and has become acclimated to her new environment, you can begin a gradual food change. Add more new food to the usual food each day until it has entirely replaced the previous diet.

LIFE-STAGE FEEDING

Puppies and adolescent dogs require a much higher intake of protein, calories and nutrients than adult dogs due to the demands of their rapidly developing bodies. Most commercial brands of dry kibble meet these requirements and are well balanced for proper growth. The majority of puppy foods now available are so carefully planned that it is unwise to add anything other than water to them.

The major ingredients of most dry dog foods are chicken, beef or lamb by-products; and corn, wheat or rice. The higher the meat content, the higher the protein percentage, palatability and digestibility of the food. Protein percentages in puppy food are usually between 25 and 30 percent. There are many advantages of dry foods over semi-moist and canned dog foods for puppies and normal, healthy adult Poms.

It is best to feed meals that are primarily dry food because the chewing action involved in eating a dry food is better for teeth and gum health. Dry food is also less expensive than canned food of equal quality.

Dogs whose diets are based on canned or soft foods have a greater likelihood of developing calcium deposits and gum disease. Canned or semimoist foods do serve certain functions, however. As a supplement to dry dog food, in small portions, canned or semimoist foods can be useful to stimulate appetites and aid in weight gain. But unless very special conditions exist, they are not the best way for a dog to meet her food needs.

A FEEDING SCHEDULE

By the time you bring your puppy home, she will probably be at the stage where three meals will suffice. Your new puppy should be fed morning, midday and evening. Fresh water should be available to her at

GROWTH STAGE FOODS

Once upon a time, there was puppy food and there was adult dog food. Now there are foods for puppies, young adults/active dogs, less active dogs and senior citizens. What's the difference between these foods? They vary by the amounts of nutrients they provide for the dog's growth stage/activity level.

Less active dogs don't need as much protein or fat as growing, active dogs; senior dogs don't need some of the nutrients vital to puppies. By feeding a high-quality food that's appropriate for your dog's age and activity level, you're benefiting your dog and yourself. Feed too much protein to a couch potato and she'll have energy to spare, which means a few more trips around the block will be needed to burn it off. Feed an adult diet to a puppy, and risk growth and development abnormalities that could affect her for a lifetime.

33

Feeding your Pomeranian dry food helps keep her teeth and gums healthy.

TO SUPPLEMENT OR NOT TO SUPPLEMENT?

If you're feeding your dog a diet that's correct for her developmental stage and she's alert, healthy looking and neither over- nor under-weight, you don't need to add supplements. These include table scraps as well as vitamins and minerals. In fact, unless you are a nutrition expert, using food supplements can actually hurt a growing puppy. For example, mixing too much calcium into your dog's food can lead to musculoskeletal disorders. Educating yourself about the quantity of vitamins and minerals your dog needs to be healthy will help you determine what needs to be supplemented. If you have any concerns about the nutritional quality of the food you're feeding, discuss them with your veterinarian.

One of the best ways to spot health problems in dogs is to monitor their food and water intake.

all times. A good plan to follow is to divide the amount recommended by the veterinarian by three. If the puppy is finishing all three of these portions throughout the day and the appearance of the body indicates proper growth, then stay with those amounts. If the puppy looks like she is gaining weight excessively, then reduce the amount that is given. The same applies for the puppy that leaves quantities of food uneaten, yet is at a good weight and energy level otherwise. Obviously, if a puppy is eating her rations and appears thin, her food intake should be increased. This is something that can only be accomplished by observation and good judgment.

From 6 months to 1 year of age, the puppy should remain on puppy food. Feedings may be reduced to twice a day if there are no hypo-glycemic problems. By the time a dog reaches 1 year of age, she should be switched to an adult maintenance diet. The number of feedings can remain at twice a day or even three times a day to ensure your Pom is breaking down sugars properly.

Puppies and dogs should have a place of their own where they can eat their meals without disturbance.

A dog's crate can be an ideal place to feed a dog. Give the dog a definite period of time to eat her food rather than allowing her to nibble throughout the day. If the food has not been eaten within a ten-minute period, pick it up and do not feed again until the next mealtime. One of the best ways to spot health problems in dogs is by monitoring their food intake.

Some owners like to add variety to their dogs' lives with human food. Table scraps, contrary to popular opinion, are not necessarily bad for your dog. The problem is what type you eat and the amount you feed. Cookies, ice cream and fatty foods will produce instant hypoglycemia in your Pom. The palatability of other types of scraps will cause your pet to eat less dog food, which results in an unhealthy diet and an overweight dog.

Pomeranians love yogurt, cottage cheese, chicken, cucumbers, broccoli, green peppers and apples. All of these choices are healthy and make good additions to the Pomeranian's diet. Avoid feeding your Pom fruits and vegetables such as grapes, tomatoes and carrots, as these foods contain sugar that will cause hypoglycemia in

HOW MANY MEALS A DAY

Individual dogs vary in how much they should eat to maintain a desired body weight—not too fat, but not too thin. Puppies need several meals a day, while older dogs may need only one. Determine how much food keeps your adult dog looking and feeling her best. Then decide how many meals you want to feed with that amount. Like us, most dogs love to eat, and offering two meals a day is more enjoyable for them. If you're worried about overfeeding, make sure you measure correctly and abstain from adding tidbits to the meals.

Whether you feed one or two meals, only leave your dog's food out for the amount of time it takes her to eat it—ten minutes, for example. Free-feeding (when food is available any time) and leisurely meals encourage picky eating. Don't worry if your dog doesn't finish all her dinner in the allotted time. She'll learn she should.

A well-fed Pom has bright eyes, a shiny coat and lots of energy.

35

How to Read the Dog Food Label

With so many choices on the market, how can you be sure you are feeding the right food to your dog? The information is all there on the label—if you know what you're looking for.

Look for the nutritional claim right up top. Is the food "100 percent nutritionally complete"? If so, it's for nearly all life stages; "growth and maintenance," on the other hand, is for early development; puppy foods are marked as such, as are foods for senior dogs.

Ingredients are listed in descending order by weight. The first three or four ingredients will tell you the bulk of what the food contains. Look for the highest-quality ingredients, like meats and grains, to be among them.

The Guaranteed Analysis tells you what levels of protein, fat, fiber and moisture are in the food, in that order. While these numbers are meaningful, they won't tell you much about the quality of the food. Nutritional value is in the dry matter, not the moisture content.

In many ways, seeing is believing. If your dog has bright eyes, a shiny coat, a good appetite and a good energy level, chances are her diet's fine. Your dog's breeder and your veterinarian are good sources of advice if you're still confused.

If you mix table scraps with dog food, and your Pom picks out each piece of kibble, licks it clean and then refuses to eat it, offer people food as "desert" when your puppy has eaten all her kibble.

Only feed healthy human food from the table if your Pom is sitting or lying down quietly. If your dog ever begs or bugs you, simply have her leave the room.

The amount of food an adult Pomeranian should eat daily will vary according to the size of the dog, her activity level and how much time she spends outside.

Most Pomeranian owners should consider placing their dog on a food that is very low in fat and protein content by the age of 8 or 9, unless the dog is still very active. A dog that is inactive either by choice or the owner's laziness has lower nutritional requirements. Another thing to keep in mind is that as dogs age, their kidneys can be destroyed if kept on a food with high protein content. Foods formulated for older dogs are low in fat and protein content.

Maintaining the proper weight and nutrition of an older Pomeranian is probably more difficult than weight maintenance at any

your Pom and make her feel hungry and gain weight.

other stage of the Pomeranian's life. A certain amount of body fat is necessary to protect her in the event of illness. Too much excess weight will make the dog even less active and more prone to physical problems. If a dog develops problems such as kidney failure, heart disease or an overly sensitive digestive tract, specially formulated foods that are commercially available might be necessary.

FOOD ALLERGIES

If your puppy or dog seems to itch all the time for no apparent reason, she could be allergic to one or more ingredients in her food. This is not uncommon, and it's why many foods contain lamb and rice instead of beef, wheat or soy. Have your dog tested by your veterinarian, and be patient while you strive to identify and eliminate the allergens from your dog's food (or environment).

This owner feeds a high quality food and keeps her Poms in optimum weight for their size. In return, she is rewarded with Pomeranians whose health and fitness mirror their diet.

CHAPTER FIVE

Putting on the Dog

A simple weekly routine can keep your Pomeranian clean, neat and free of tangles. Besides having cosmetic benefits, grooming can be a pleasant experience for your dog and will strengthen the bond between you.

SUPPLIES

The minimum supplies needed are: a pin brush, a slicker brush, a metal comb made for dogs, 4-inch ball-tipped scissors and cat nail clippers. You also will need baby powder, a

plastic spray bottle and grooming spray. Talcum powder can be dangerous for your Pom to breathe, so make sure the baby powder you buy is made of 100 percent cornstarch. For a grooming mist, use plain water or one of the following mixtures.

Mixture one:

One tablespoon of cream rinse. Get the kind made for dogs.

Eight ounces of water.

Mix ingredients together and fill the spray bottle.

Mixture two:

One to two tablespoons of Eau de Quinine Compound Hair Tonic by Ed Pinaud. This is a men's hair tonic, bright red in color, that can be purchased in most drugstore chains.

Six ounces of water.

A dash of witch hazel (optional).

BRUSHING

Never brush a dry coat, as this will break off the ends of the hair. Use the spray bottle filled with plain water or one of the grooming

GROOMING TOOLS

pin brush	scissors
slicker brush	nail clippers
flea comb	tooth-cleaning equipment
towel	shampoo
mat rake	conditioner
grooming glove	clippers

Grooming is a great way to bond with your Pom.

39

mixtures. Before you start brushing, dust some of the baby powder behind the ears and leave it there. This soaks up the oil that builds up in this area. Use a grooming table to brush your dog, but if you don't have one, don't worry; your lap will work just as well.

Use a slicker brush to remove any remnants of baby powder or mats from your dog's coat.

Find a comfortable chair, cover your legs with a towel, and lay the dog in your lap. Put the dog on his side, head toward your knees, rump toward your body. Spritz some water or grooming mixture on him and, starting near the rump, separate the hair until you see the skin. Hold the top section down with one hand, and brush the bottom section in the direction the hair grows. Move up an inch and separate another section of hair, and repeat. Keep moving forward an inch or so until you have brushed his whole side. Repeat on the other side, then place him on his back. If you have a male, moisten the gummy area on his belly with the spray, then powder heavily and brush out the powder with the slicker brush. You may have to mist and powder this area more than once. When finished, switch back to the pin brush and groom the chest, under the legs, his back and the breast area under his chin.

Change over to the slicker brush and brush out the baby powder around the ears. If you find tangles, use your fingers to pull them apart, and starting near the skin, cut through the mat out to the end of the hair. Use the metal comb to remove the cut sections.

Finally, switch back to the pin brush, mist his coat and lightly brush his whole body, going against the grain and fluffing his hair toward his head. Put him on the floor and he will give a shake that settles each hair in place.

TRIMMING

The Pom can get feces stuck in his coat. To avoid this, take the blunt scissors and trim a small area, about

Unless he has an unusually heavy coat, your Pom only needs to be brushed once a week.

41

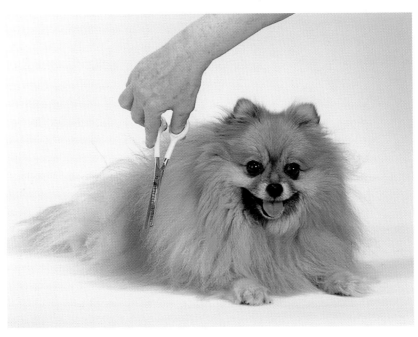

Scissors like these help put the finishing touches on your Pom's coat, feet and ears.

one inch in diameter, around the anal opening.

When the hair between the Pom's toes becomes too long, it interferes with his ability to walk on slippery floors. Turn the dog over on his back, and using the blunt scissors, carefully cut the hair between the toes.

Stand your Pom on a table or other hard surface, and, trimming around the foot, remove the tuft of hair that grows in front of the toes. Some pet owners leave this tuft, while others prefer the look of the trimmed foot.

Depending on your preference, the hair on the tips of the ears can be left natural or trimmed. Place the

Pom in a sitting position with his head facing you. Grasp the ear at the top, putting the ear leather between your thumb and first finger. Make sure you are covering the ear-tip with your fingernails. Cut straight across the tip, then cut, at a slight angle downward, $1/4$ inch on each side. Repeat on the other ear.

BATHING

If you brush your Pom once a week, you should rarely have to give him a bath. If a bath does become necessary, you can bathe him in your kitchen sink. He may become frightened of the slippery bottom, so

This good boy was trained at an early age to sit calmly for his nail trim.

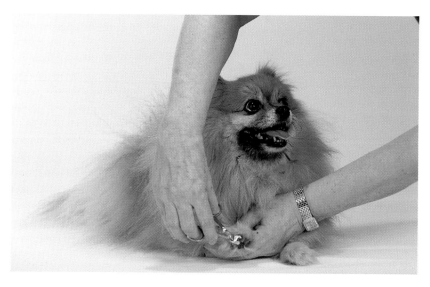

put a rubber mat under his feet. Before you place your dog in the sink, turn on the water and adjust the temperature. Using the sink hose, wet him down until his coat is saturated.

After he is thoroughly wet, move the running faucet out of his way but do not turn it off. It is difficult to adjust the water temperature with a wet, soapy Pom in the sink, so once you have the warm/cold ratio correct, let the water run during the whole bath. Sometime during the wetting process, the Pom will try to shake his wet coat. When this happens, grab the skin at the base of his neck and he will stop shaking.

Start at the neck area and apply enough shampoo to work up a lather. Be careful not to get any in his eyes. Work the lather into the hair and then thoroughly rinse. Wrap him in a thick towel and wipe off all excess water. Use a paper towel to wipe away any moisture in his ears, then blow-dry the coat.

Except for the insecticidal brands, your choice of shampoo is a matter of personal choice. Strong flea shampoos can harm the tiny Pom, so it is important that you follow the directions on the label, and use insecticidal shampoos purchased

QUICK AND PAINLESS NAIL CLIPPING

This is possible if you make a habit out of handling your dog's feet and giving your dog treats when you do. When it's time to clip nails, go through the same routine, but take your clippers and snip off just the ends of the nail—clip too far down and you'll cut into the "quick," the nerve center, hurting your dog and causing the nail to bleed. Clip two nails a session while you're getting your dog used to the procedure, and you'll soon be doing all four feet quickly and easily.

43

from pet stores or your veterinarian, rather than supermarkets. Never use a shampoo designed for human use on your Pom, as this can cause his skin to become dry and itchy.

Blow-Drying

The Pomeranian's coat must be blown dry—even in the summer. The undercoat is too thick to dry quickly, and in hot, humid weather, a wet undercoat can cause hot spots to develop.

Place your dog on your lap, hold the hair dryer about ten inches away from his body, and, taking care to avoid his face, blow-dry the coat for

Your Pom requires good dental hygiene, just like humans, to keep his teeth healthy and his breath fresh.

TEETH

Hard kibble and nylon chew toys should keep your Pom's teeth white, but sometimes it's not enough to do the job. For optimal tartar prevention, brush at least three times a week using an infant toothbrush or one made especially for dogs. You also can use a toothpaste made for dogs, but plain water will work as well. Just make sure you never use human toothpaste; it will make your dog sick.

about two minutes. Turn the dryer off and brush him with the pin brush, then blow another few minutes, and brush again. Keep this up until he is dry.

EARS

During the weekly grooming, check the inside of your Pom's ears for any

Remember to check inside your Pomeranian's ears to make sure that they are clean and dry.

kind of wax buildup or dark, brownish discharge.

SHEDDING

The Pomeranian sheds between 4 and 6 months of age, and again when he is 1 year old. After that, the male sheds once a year, and the female at each season. Good grooming practices will keep these shedding episodes short.

Poms shed their coat in two different ways, and each type requires a different grooming method. Some Poms blow their coat all at once with large clumps of hair separating from the body. Brush out the clumps with the slicker brush, bathe, blow-dry and brush again. You must brush the dog before his bath; otherwise, the undercoat will form felt-like mats. Repeat this process a week later and you should find that most of the shed is finished. When you sit down to brush the dog, make sure you have a paper

A clean, well-groomed Pom is a pleasure to look at.

bag next to you for receiving the dead coat.

In the second type of shed, the hair doesn't clump but falls out continuously. Bathe the dog, blow-dry and for the next two weeks brush daily. Don't make it a long process; just do a light brushing to pull out the dead hair. Other than the shedding period, fifteen minutes once a week is all the time needed to keep your Pomeranian well groomed.

CHAPTER SIX

Measuring Up

WHAT IS THE STANDARD AND WHY DO WE NEED IT?

All purebred dogs are created artificially. When man discovered that he had more to eat because his floppy-eared, liver-and-white dog pointed at quail, he conscientiously bred to retain these traits. Selective breeding is how every purebred dog got her start, but breeders, being human, did not all agree on what traits to reproduce. Different owners would make parentage choices that had the potential to drastically change or hinder the development of the breed. For instance, in making the Pom smaller, breeders would mate small size to small size, but some considered fifteen pounds small, and others, five pounds. Therefore, in order to create and preserve the breeds, the breeders needed guidance as to what traits, structure and type to cultivate.

They acquired the needed guidance by forming organized breed clubs. Members of these clubs then compiled written descriptions, called breed standards, of the perfect representative of their breed. Early breeders used these standards as blueprints for their breeding programs, and with few revisions, they are still used today. Many local clubs represent a breed, but only the national breed club, called the parent club, decides standard revisions. In the United States, the American Pomeranian Club is the parent club that guards the breed ideal for the Pomeranian.

The breed standard depicts the perfect dog—a concept to work for—it doesn't mean something is wrong if your pet doesn't conform to the Standard. Even top show dogs don't measure up to the model in every way. So if your Suzie-Q has ears like a jackrabbit, and the Standard calls

WHAT IS A BREED STANDARD?

A breed standard—a detailed description of an individual breed—is meant to portray the ideal specimen of that breed. This includes ideal structure, temperament, gait, type—all aspects of the dog. Because the standard describes an ideal specimen, it isn't based on any particular dog. It is a concept against which judges compare actual dogs and breeders strive to produce dogs. At a dog show, the dog that wins is the one that comes closest, in the judge's opinion, to the standard for its breed. Breed standards are written by the breed parent clubs, the national organizations formed to oversee the well-being of the breed. They are voted on and approved by the members of the parent clubs.

47

for tiny ears, don't get upset; she's as good as any other Pom, but to preserve breed type you wouldn't mate her to a dog that also sported jackrabbit ears—in fact, you wouldn't mate her at all. Remember, if breeders mated purebred dogs indiscriminately, breed types would disappear.

STUDYING THE STANDARD

Since the Pomeranian is a companion dog, the standard ranks temperament and appearance high in importance. It also calls for soundness. As a smaller version of the Nordic dog, the Pomeranian, if enlarged, should be able to pull a sled and work in snow. The standard is in italics, and the author's comments follow.

General Appearance

The Pomeranian in build and appearance is a cobby, balanced and short-coupled dog. He exhibits great intelligence in expression and is alert in character and deportment.

This section calls for a cobby, balanced dog, but it may leave you

The Pom's alertness makes her a great watchdog.

wondering what cobby means or how to define balance. A cobby dog is as tall or taller as she is long; try to picture her as a circle in a square. A balanced Pomeranian fits together logically and in proportion. For instance, a small, delicately boned Pom with a large, coarse head looks unbalanced because her head type doesn't match her body type. A balanced Pom displays legs in proportion to her body: neither so short as to make her appear dumpy nor so long as to make her look like she is walking on stilts.

The general appearance segment also calls for an expression that imparts great intelligence. It tells us the Pom has an alert character and that she behaves accordingly. A stupid or dull Pom would not make a good comrade, so intelligence is an essential trait for this breed. Her alertness not only makes her a superb watchdog, but adds to the "I'm special" attitude she exhibits.

Size, Proportion and Substance

Size: The weight of the Pomeranian for exhibition is from three to seven pounds. The ideal size for show specimens is four to five pounds.

The Pomeranian's size ranges from three to seven pounds, and her facial type can vary as well.

Proportion: The Pomeranian in build and appearance is a cobby, balanced, short coupled dog. The legs are of medium length in proportion to a well balanced frame.

Substance: The body is well ribbed and rounded. The brisket is fairly deep and not too wide.

The standard calls for a dog that weighs from three to seven pounds. This broad weight range allows a dramatic difference in appearance to occur between a three-pounder and a seven-pounder. According to the standard, both sizes are equal. The preferred weight of the Pom is in the middle of these two extremes—four to five pounds.

The proportions of the Pomeranian make her look fit the circle-in-a-square image. Measure the length of the dog from her shoulders to the root of the tail and the height from the shoulders to the ground. A dog with proper proportion is as long or shorter than she is tall. Her chest, called the brisket, goes deep enough to reach the elbow. Her well-rounded body is not too wide, but has substance.

Head

Well proportioned to the body, wedge-shaped, with a fox-like expression.

Eyes: Bright, dark in color, and medium in size, almond-shaped and

This Pom flashes her baby-doll face.

50

not set too far apart nor too close together. Pigmentation around eye rims must be black, except self-colored in brown and blue.

Ears: Small, carried erect and mounted high on the head placed not too far apart.

Skull: Not domed in outline. A round, domey skull is a major fault.

Muzzle: There is a pronounced stop with a rather fine but not snipy muzzle. Pigment around the lips must be black, except self-colored in brown and blue.

Bite: The teeth meet in a scissors bite in which part of the inner surface of the upper teeth meet and engages part of the outer surface of the lower

teeth. One tooth out of line does not mean an undershot or overshot mouth. An undershot mouth is a major fault.

Nose: Pigment on the nose must be black, except self colored in brown and blue.

The standard calls for a wedge-shaped head but does not define the width of the wedge. Keep in mind that a narrow wedge makes the head look like a Sheltie's and a wide wedge will give the Pom a Chow Chow appearance. The correct wedge falls in the middle range and helps keep the Pomeranian head from developing a dwarfing effect.

A side effect of breeding dogs down to a tiny size is the tendency for small dogs to take on dwarf-like features, such as a flattened muzzle, bulging round eyes, domed heads, bowed legs and heavier bone. The developers of breeds like the Pug, Pekingese and Brussels Griffon used this tendency to their advantage. Some Poms display a sweet face, with round eyes, rounder skull and shortened muzzle, called a baby-doll face.

Continued breeding of this admittedly precious look would eventually give the Pom a Pekingese face. The standard guides us away from this dwarfing effect by requiring a wedge-shaped, undomed head with a pronounced stop.

The standard calls for a fox-like expression, and the important word to remember here is "expression."

The Bite, Eyes and Ears sections read reasonably clearly. Recognize that the almond-shaped eyes and small high-set ears add to the fox-like expression.

Neck, Topline and Body

Neck: The neck is rather short, its base set well back on the shoulders.

Topline is level.

Body: The body is cobby, being well ribbed and rounded.

Chest: The brisket is fairly deep and not too wide.

Tail: The tail is a characteristic of the breed. It turns over the back and is carried flat, set high.

The Neck, Topline and Body segment states that the Pomeranian's neck is set well back on the shoulders, which allows for that proud carriage of the head that shows her jaunty "I can" attitude. A Pom with a neck that is not set well back will carry her head forward as she walks. The proper set and carriage of the tail creates the essential look of the Pom. A tail set up high and flat on the back with the feathering touching the neck ruff pulls

The Pom does not look like a long-muzzled, big-eared fox, but exhibits the quick, alert, watchful expression of one.

51

THE AMERICAN KENNEL CLUB

Familiarly referred to as "the AKC," the American Kennel Club is a nonprofit organization devoted to the advancement of purebred dogs. The AKC maintains a registry of recognized breeds and adopts and enforces rules for dog events including shows, obedience trials, field trials, hunting tests, lure coursing, herding, earthdog trials, agility and the Canine Good Citizen program. It is a club of clubs, established in 1884 and composed, today, of over 500 autonomous dog clubs throughout the United States. Each club is represented by a delegate; the delegates make up the legislative body of the AKC, voting on rules and electing directors. The American Kennel Club maintains the Stud Book, the record of every dog ever registered with the AKC, and publishes a variety of materials on purebred dogs, including a monthly magazine, books and numerous educational pamphlets. For more information, contact the AKC at the address listed in Chapter 9, "Resources."

the appearance of the Pom into a circle. A low-set tail makes the Pom look long and gives her a rectangular appearance. Some tails curl, and while the standard doesn't address this, a tight curl takes away from the desired circle appearance. The curl may even cause the tail to lay to the side of the dog's body.

Forequarters

Shoulders: The Pomeranian is not straight in shoulder, but has sufficient layback of shoulders to carry the neck proudly and high.

Forelegs: The forelegs are straight and parallel, of medium length in proportion to a well balanced frame.

Pasterns: The Pomeranian stands well up on toes. Down in pasterns is a major fault.

Dewclaws: Dewclaws on the forelegs may be removed.

Feet: The Pomeranian stands well up on toes.

Hindquarters

Angulation: Hindquarters and forequarters should be of equal angulation.

Legs: The hocks are perpendicular to the ground, parallel to each other from hock to heel, and turning neither in nor out. Cow hocks or lack of soundness in hind legs or stifles is a major fault. Dewclaws, if any, on the hind legs are generally removed.

In the Forequarter and Hindquarter sections, notice the emphasis on soundness in the Pomeranian's legs. Remember the Pom, if enlarged, should be like any other Nordic dog. Small size is not an excuse to accept bad stifles or lame legs. Today's Pom may not be a working dog, but she still needs strong healthy legs to run and play. After all, how can she be a lapdog unless her legs are hardy enough to allow her to jump on your lap? Straight, parallel legs present efficient movement. A Pom who stands well up on her toes has cat-shaped feet that almost disappear in her fur.

Coat

Coat type on head, legs and tail differs from body coat.

Head coat: Head coat is tightly packed and shorter in length than that of the body.

Body coat: Double coated; a short, soft, thick coat consisting of guard hairs, which must be harsh to the touch in order to give the proper texture for the coat to form a frill of profuse, stand-off, straight hair. A soft, flat or open coat is a major fault.

Tail coat: It is profusely covered with hair.

Leg coat: The front legs are well feathered and the hindquarters are clad with long hair or feathering from the top of the rump to the hocks.

Trimming: Trimming for neatness is permissible around the feet and up the back of the legs to the first joint; trimming of unruly hairs on the edges of the ears and around the anus is also permitted. Overtrimming (beyond the

The harsh outer coat of the Pomeranian repels water and snow and keeps her warm.

Your Pom is a loving and loyal pet even if she doesn't perfectly fit the breed standard.

location and amount described in the breed Standard) should be heavily penalized.

The Coat section reflects the Pom's Nordic ancestry, and of all the elements in the standard, this is, other than size, the one that most defines his look. The harsh outer coat repels water and snow, and the dense undercoat keeps her warm. This type of coat does not lay flat, or split down the middle, but stands off from the body, giving the Pom her round, majestic look. The proper coat tangles less and is easier to groom. The standard uses the word "harsh" to describe the texture of the guard hairs, but the outer coat doesn't really feel hard to the touch.

The hairs feel tougher than the undercoat, but not as hard as a wire-haired coat.

Color

Classifications: The open classes at Specialty shows may be divided by color as follows: Open Red, Orange, Cream, Sable; Open Black, Brown and Blue; Open Any Other Allowed Color.

Acceptable colors to be judged on an equal basis. Any solid color, any solid color with lighter or darker shadings of the same color, any solid color with sable or black shadings, parti-color, sable and black and tan. Black and tan is black with tan or rust, sharply defined, appearing above each eye and on the muzzle, throat and forechest, on all legs and feet and below the tail. Parti-color is white with any other color distributed in even patches on the body and a white blaze on the head. A white chest, foot or leg on a whole-colored dog (except white) is a major fault.

COLOR—The color section of the standard causes the most confusion to Pom owners. This breed comes in a variety of colors and shades and sometimes it is difficult to know what a certain color, such as beaver, looks like, or whether or not a color fits the rules of the standard. In studying this section, let's start with the acceptable color definitions. Any solid color: Red, orange, black, blue, chocolate, cream, white and beaver all fit this category.

RED—Often dark oranges are mistakenly called red. A true red comes close to a rich Irish Setter color.

ORANGE—A clear bright color, and currently the most popular of Pomeranian colors. Orange ranges from a deep rust through a rich gold to a blond shade. Breeders prefer the deep gold over the washed-out blond shade.

BLACK—The glimmer of a rich, blue-black sheen is more desirable than a coat dusted with a rusty tint.

BLUE—A rather rare color today, blue is hard to describe. It is a slate gray color with more of a bluish tint than a gray one. A blue dog must have a blue nose.

CHOCOLATE—This color looks like rich chocolate in hue; the dog's nose also must show the chocolate color.

CREAM—The cream color flows evenly throughout the coat with no shades of white or yellow. Black-tipped hairs on the coat make the dog a cream sable.

55

A red Pomeranian.

A cream sable Pomeranian sits to the left of a cream Pom.

WHITE—A pure snow-white color with no shades of yellow behind the ears or on the coat. The nose and eye rims on a white dog must be black.

A black and tan Pom.

BEAVER—A very rare color, beaver has been called everything from washed-out chocolate to beige. This color is sort of a pale, soft, grayish-beige, taupelike hue. The dog's nose should be the same shade.

ANY SOLID COLOR WITH LIGHTER OR DARKER SHADINGS OF THE SAME COLOR—Orange dogs darker on the back, with the color lighter under the tail and on the chest, fit in this category. So would a red with orange breeches, as orange is a dilution of red. Note that the color, though lighter, must be the same hue. An orange dog with white under the tail or chest is two colors and would be considered a mismark.

ANY SOLID COLOR WITH SABLE OR BLACK SHADINGS—Any color, cream, orange, gray, etc., with black shadings. This includes a black mask, black saddle and black tips to the guard hairs. Some dogs may display a clear orange with only the back and the mask showing black, and some, called shaded sables, may have sabling throughout the coat.

BLACK AND TAN AND PARTI-COLORS—This section reads reasonably clearly and doesn't need further elaboration, except to note that the color patches on a parti-color can be any color.

BRINDLE, CHOCOLATE AND TAN, BLUE AND TAN—These three colors may or may not be classified as acceptable colors as per the standard. It all depends on how you interpret it. Therefore, some judges penalize these colors and others award them the ribbon. Chocolate and tan could technically be defined as a solid color with lighter shadings, blue and tan could be defined as a diluted black and tan, and many claim the brindles are solid colors

with black shadings. Others claim these colors don't belong because the standard doesn't clearly describe them. Whatever the viewpoint, the current standard does not disqualify any dog for deviation of color.

Gait

The Pomeranian moves with a smooth, free but not loose action. He does not elbow out in front nor move excessively wide nor cow-hocked behind. He is sound in action.

The Pom with a proper gait doesn't bounce up and down, lift her front legs with a bent knee or move with her legs real close together. She covers ground in a smooth action with front legs that reach out as far as her nose and hind legs that drive hard from the rear.

Temperament

He exhibits great intelligence in expression, and is alert in character and deportment.

Brave, sweet and loving, the Pomeranian will dedicate herself to her owner; friendly, intelligent and classy, she is also a character; one who thinks she can.

CHAPTER SEVEN

A Matter of Fact

THE POMERANIAN TODAY

From a beloved companion of royalty to the playmate of Ziegfeld girls, the Pom always mingled with the rich and famous, and today's Pomeranian follows this tradition. Poms appeared in the biographical movie *Liberace* and in the television series *The Nanny.* Champion Great Elm's Prince Charming II, the Pom who won Westminster in 1988, topped his show ring career with a stint in show business. For several years, he starred in television commercials as a representative of a dog food company.

In appearance, the modern Pomeranian resembles his ancestors, but at the same time he looks vastly different. Occasionally, a larger dog of the older type may appear in a litter, but the breed today is truly a toy breed, and Poms usually weigh under seven pounds. He also comes in a variety of colors to satisfy every taste.

Regardless of color, the popularity of the Pomeranian flourishes. Bearing the title of "companion dog," he has left the cold halls of castles for the comfort of central heating and is now firmly ensconced in homes around the world.

Although his ancestors were much larger dogs, today's Pomeranian is truly a toy breed.

EARLY HISTORY

The Pomeranian goes far back in history. Over 10,000 years ago, a Spitz type of dog, the first of the Nordic group, made its appearance. These northern forest dogs, believed to be the first type of dog associated with man, include the Akita, Malamute, Norwegian Elkhound, Samoyed, Keeshond, Chow Chow, Finnish Spitz, Schipperke and Pomeranian.

Curled tails (except for the Schipperke), erect ears, dense undercoats and harsh outer coats characterize the Nordic group. Members of this group closely resemble each other, and the Pom looks like a smaller version of a Keeshond, Elkhound or Samoyed.

The earlier Pomeranians differed in appearance from our current tiny version; they weighed between thirty and thirty-five pounds, with larger ears, longer muzzles and longer backs. They didn't have the wide variety of colors of our present-day Pom. White or biscuit seemed to be the most common color, with some black, blue and brown dogs.

Along with the rest of the Nordic group, the Pomeranian herded animals and pulled sleds, but even during the plebeian years of his history he managed to associate with the elite. Greek pottery portrays the Pom romping with Apollo

WHERE DID DOGS COME FROM?

It can be argued that dogs were right there at man's side from the beginning of time. As soon as human beings began to document their existence, the dog was among their drawings and inscriptions. Dogs were not just friends, they served a purpose: There were dogs to hunt birds, pull sleds, herd sheep, burrow after rats—even sit in laps! What your dog was originally bred to do influences the way he behaves. The American Kennel Club recognizes over 140 breeds, and there are hundreds more distinct breeds around the world. To make sense of the breeds, they are grouped according to their size or function. The AKC has seven groups:

1. Sporting
2. Working
3. Herding
4. Hounds
5. Terriers
6. Toys
7. Non Sporting

Can you name a breed from each group? Here's some help: (1) Golden Retriever, (2) Doberman Pinscher, (3) Collie, (4) Beagle, (5) Scottish Terrier, (6) Maltese, and (7) Dalmatian. All modern domestic dogs (*Canis familiaris*) are related, however different they look, and are all descended from *Canis lupus*, the gray wolf.

and Aphrodite, and drawings of him appear in tombs made for Egyptian kings. Sometime before 1872, the Pom left his working background to join dogdom's leisure classes and became strictly a companion.

THE ENGLISH BACKGROUND

The first Pomeranians brought into England came from a northeast corner of Germany called Pomerania. Although they are named after it, Poms did not develop in this province, but actually originated in southern Germany.

Occasionally these larger Pomeranians whelped a litter that contained a sport: an extra-small puppy. At maturity these puppies weighed about ten to twelve pounds, a drastic difference from the thirty-pound parents. The adorable appearance of the sports created an interest in them. This and the public's interest in the diminutive version of the Pomeranian (popularized by Queen Victoria) led to deliberate breeding for the smaller size.

Fanciers reduced size successfully, and by the 1890s the size of Pomeranians entered at English Kennel Club shows was much

Before he became a companion dog for the elite, the Pomeranian actually herded animals and pulled sleds.

smaller. In 1896, two size categories appeared for Pomeranians: over eight pounds and under eight pounds. Eventually the categories changed to over or under seven pounds. Finally, as breeders successfully made the Pomeranian a toy dog, the over-seven-pound category disappeared altogether.

POMERANIANS IN THE UNITED STATES

The earliest mention of Pomeranians in the United States appeared in the late 1880s when the American Kennel Club (AKC) registered the first one. The initial imports, large white Poms weighing around twenty to thirty pounds, came from England. At first, fanciers brought them over for use in the show ring, but the breed quickly spread throughout the United States to rule ordinary households.

In 1900, the AKC recognized the Pomeranian with the result that, at dog shows, the Pom could now leave the miscellaneous classes and exhibit in the Non-Sporting Group. He remained in this group until the establishment of the Toy Group in 1928. The standard at this time, similar to England's, called for under- and over-eight-pound categories, so as late as the early 1930s the larger Pomeranians remained.

FAMOUS OWNERS OF POMERANIANS

Fran Drescher	Michelangelo
David Hasselhoff	Isaac Newton
Queen Victoria	

The same year that the AKC recognized the breed, Mrs. Frank Smyth and Mrs. Hartley Williamson founded the American Pomeranian Club (APC), and nine years later the club became a member of the AKC. They founded the club as a way to promote the breeding of purebred Pomeranians and to urge members to follow the APC Standard of Excellence in breeding.

The first Pomeranians in America were imported from England and weighed between twenty and thirty pounds.

The members of APC guard the breed standard and determine what changes, if any, occur in it. In 1911, the APC held its first specialty show. For the past thirty years, this affair, held the day before the Westminster Kennel Club show, has taken place in New York.

HISTORY OF POMERANIAN COLORS

During the late 1890s, Pomeranian coats were white, black, brown, blue, dark orange, beaver, cream, particolor and shaded sable. As the breed became smaller, the white color went out of favor. It is difficult to breed white Poms and still keep them small. The gene for a white-colored coat seems to be linked to the gene for a bigger size, and if you breed white dogs to white dogs, the offspring start to revert to a larger Pom with bigger ears and longer muzzles.

The flashy, brilliant, clear orange became the rage during this century, almost obliterating the other colors, and by the 1980s the other colors, except for orange sable, seemed to disappear. Fortunately, in the last ten years the trend reversed, and now it is common to see cream, cream sable, black, black and tan, parti-color and chocolate Poms; less so the beaver, blue and white colors, but they are out there. The wolf sable, however, is extremely rare. When an advertisement lists this color, be assured these people do not know much about the Pomeranian. They confuse the normal grayish-brown puppy hue, which will mature to an orange color, with the black-tipped, silver wolf, sable color.

Pomeranians come in an array of colors.

63

CHAPTER EIGHT

On Good Behavior

by Ian Dunbar, Ph.D., MRCVS

Training is the jewel in the crown—the most important aspect of doggy husbandry. There is no more important variable influencing dog behavior and temperament than the dog's education: A well-trained, well-behaved and good-natured puppydog is always a joy to live with, but an untrained and uncivilized dog can be a perpetual nightmare. Moreover, deny the dog an education and she will not have the opportunity to fulfill her own canine potential; neither will she have the ability to communicate effectively with her human companions.

Luckily, modern psychological training methods are easy, efficient, effective and, above all, considerably dog-friendly and user-friendly. Doggy education is as simple as it is enjoyable. But before you can have a good time play-training with your new dog, you have to learn what to do and how to do it. There is no bigger variable influencing the success of dog training than the owner's experience and expertise. Before you embark on the dog's education, you must first educate yourself.

BASIC TRAINING FOR OWNERS

Ideally, basic owner training should begin well before you select your dog. Find out all you can about your chosen breed first, then master rudimentary training and handling skills. If you already have your puppydog, owner training is a dire emergency—the clock is ticking! Especially for puppies, the first few weeks at home are the most important and influential days in the dog's life. Indeed, the cause of most adolescent and adult problems may be traced back to the initial days the pup explores her new home. This is the time to establish the *status quo*—

to teach the puppydog how you would like her to behave and so prevent otherwise quite predictable problems.

In addition to consulting breeders and breed books such as this one (which understandably have a positive breed bias), seek out as many pet owners with your breed as you can find. Good points are obvious. What you want to find out are the breed-specific problems, so you can nip them in the bud. In particular, you should talk to owners with adolescent dogs and make a list of all anticipated problems. Most important, test drive at least half a dozen adolescent and adult dogs of your breed yourself. An 8-week-old puppy is deceptively easy to handle, but she will acquire adult size, speed and strength in just four months, so you should learn now what to prepare for.

Puppy and pet dog training classes offer a convenient venue to locate pet owners and observe dogs in action. For a list of suitable trainers in your area, contact the Association of Pet Dog Trainers (see chapter 9). You may also begin your basic owner training by observing other owners in class. Watch as many classes and test drive as many

65

dogs as possible. Select an upbeat, dog-friendly, people-friendly, fun-and-games, puppydog pet training class to learn the ropes. Also, watch training videos and read training books. You must find out what to do and how to do it *before* you have to do it.

PRINCIPLES OF TRAINING

Most people think training comprises teaching the dog to do things such as sit, speak and roll over, but even a 4-week-old pup knows how to do these things already. Instead, the first step in training involves teaching the dog human words for each dog behavior and activity and for each aspect of the dog's environment. That way you, the owner, can more easily participate in the dog's domestic education by directing her to perform specific actions appropriately, that is, at the right time, in the right place and so on. Training opens communication channels, enabling an educated dog to at least understand her owner's requests.

In addition to teaching a dog what we want her to do, it is also necessary to teach her why she should do what we ask. Indeed, 95 percent of training revolves around motivating the dog to want to do what we want. Dogs often

Deciding how you plan to train your pup before she comes home with you will help training go smoothly.

understand what their owners want; they just don't see the point of doing it—especially when the owner's repetitively boring and seemingly senseless instructions are totally at odds with much more pressing and exciting doggy distractions. It is not so much the dog that is being stubborn or dominant; rather, it is the owner who has failed to acknowledge the dog's needs and feelings and to approach training from the dog's point of view.

The Meaning of Instructions

The secret to successful training is learning how to use training lures to predict or prompt specific behaviors—to coax the dog to do what you want when you want. Any highly valued object (such as a treat or toy) may be used as a lure, which the dog will follow with her eyes and nose. Moving the lure in specific ways entices the dog to move her nose, head and entire body in specific ways. In fact, by learning the art of manipulating various lures, it is possible to teach the dog to assume virtually any body position and perform any action. Once you have control

---

OWNING A PARTY ANIMAL

It's a fact: The more of the world your puppy is exposed to, the more comfortable she'll be in it. Once your puppy's had her shots, start taking her everywhere with you. Encourage friendly interaction with strangers, expose her to different environments (towns, fields, beaches) and most important, enroll her in a puppy class where she'll get to play with other puppies. These simple, fun, shared activities will develop your pup into a confident socialite; reliable around other people and dogs.

---

over the expression of the dog's behaviors and can elicit any body position or behavior at will, you can easily teach the dog to perform on request.

Tell your dog what you want her to do, use a lure to entice her to respond correctly, then profusely praise and maybe reward her once she performs the desired action. For example, verbally request "Fido, sit!" while you move a squeaky toy upwards and backwards over the dog's muzzle (lure-movement and hand signal), smile knowingly as she looks up (to follow the lure) and sits down (as a result of canine anatomical engineering), then praise her to distraction ("Gooood Fido!").

Squeak the toy, offer a training treat and give your dog and yourself a pat on the back.

Being able to elicit desired responses over and over enables the owner to reward the dog over and over. Consequently, the dog begins to think training is fun. For example, the more the dog is rewarded for sitting, the more she enjoys sitting. Eventually the dog comes to realize that, whereas most sitting is appreciated, sitting immediately upon request usually prompts especially enthusiastic praise and a slew of high-level rewards. The dog

68

This Pom stands on her hind legs for a food reward.

begins to sit on cue much of the time, showing that she is starting to grasp the meaning of the owner's verbal request and hand signal.

Why Comply?

Most dogs enjoy initial lure-reward training and are only too happy to comply with their owners' wishes. Unfortunately, repetitive drilling without appreciative feedback tends to diminish the dog's enthusiasm until she eventually fails to see the point of complying anymore. Moreover, as the dog approaches adolescence she becomes more easily distracted as she develops other interests. Lengthy sessions with repetitive exercises tend to bore and demotivate both parties. If it's not fun, the owner doesn't do it and neither does the dog.

Integrate training into your dog's life: The greater number of training sessions each day and the shorter they are, the more willingly compliant your dog will become. Make sure to have a short (just a few seconds) training interlude before every enjoyable canine activity. For example, ask your dog to sit to greet people, to sit before you throw her Frisbee and to sit for her supper.

Really, sitting is no different from a canine "Please." Also, include numerous short training interludes during every enjoyable canine pastime, for example, when playing with the dog or when she is running in the park. In this fashion, doggy distractions may be effectively converted into rewards for training. Just as all games have rules, fun becomes training . . . and training becomes fun.

Eventually, rewards actually become unnecessary to continue motivating your dog. If trained with consideration and kindness, performing the desired behaviors will become self-rewarding and, in a sense, your dog will motivate herself. Just as it is not necessary to reward a human companion during an enjoyable walk in the park, or following a game of tennis, it is hardly necessary to reward our best friend—the dog—for walking by our side or while playing fetch. Human company during enjoyable activities is reward enough for most dogs.

Even though your dog has become self-motivating, it's still good to praise and pet her a lot and offer rewards once in a while, especially for a job well done. And if for no other reason, praising and

rewarding others is good for the human heart.

Punishment

Without a doubt, lure-reward training is by far the best way to teach: Entice your dog to do what you want and then reward her for doing so. Unfortunately, a human shortcoming is to take the good for granted and to moan and groan at the bad. Specifically, the dog's many good behaviors are ignored while the owner focuses on punishing the dog for making mistakes. In extreme cases, instruction is limited to punishing mistakes made by a trainee dog, child, employee or husband, even though it has been proven punishment training is notoriously inefficient and ineffective and is decidedly unfriendly and combative. It teaches the dog that training is a drag, almost as quickly as it teaches the dog to dislike her trainer. Why treat our best friends like our worst enemies?

Punishment training is also much more laborious and time consuming. Whereas it takes only a finite amount of time to teach a dog what to chew, for example, it takes much, much longer to punish the dog for each and every mistake. Remember, there is only one right way! So why not teach that right way from the outset?!

TRAINER'S TOOLS

Many training books extol the virtues of a vast array of training paraphernalia and electronic and metallic gizmos, most of which are designed for canine restraint, correction and punishment, rather than for actual facilitation of doggy education. In reality, most effective training tools are not found in stores; they come from within ourselves. In addition to a willing dog, all you really need is a functional human brain, gentle hands, a loving heart and a good attitude.

In terms of equipment, all dogs do require a quality buckle collar to sport dog tags and to attach the leash (for safety and to comply with local leash laws). Hollow chew toys (like Kongs or sterilized longbones) and a dog bed or collapsible crate are musts for housetraining. Three additional tools are required:

1. specific lures (training treats and toys) to predict and prompt specific desired behaviors;

2. rewards (praise, affection, training treats and toys) to reinforce for the dog what a lot of fun it all is; and

3. knowledge—how to convert the dog's favorite activities and games (potential distractions to training) into "life-rewards," which may be employed to facilitate training.

The most powerful of these is knowledge. Education is the key! Watch training classes, participate in training classes, watch videos, read books, enjoy play-training with your dog and then your dog will say "Please," and your dog will say "Thank you!"

HOUSETRAINING

If dogs were left to their own devices, certainly they would chew, dig and bark for entertainment and then no doubt highlight a few areas of their living space with sprinkles of urine, in much the same way we decorate by hanging pictures. Consequently, when we ask a dog to live with us, we must teach her *where* she may dig, *where* she may perform her toilet duties, *what* she may chew and *when* she may bark. After all, when left at home alone for many hours, we cannot expect the dog to amuse herself by completing crosswords or watching TV!

Also, it would be decidedly unfair to keep the house rules a secret from the dog, and then get angry and punish the poor critter for inevitably transgressing rules she did not even know existed. Remember: Without adequate education and guidance, the dog will be forced to establish her own rules—doggy rules—and most probably will be at odds with the owner's view of domestic living.

Since most problems develop during the first few days the dog is at home, prospective dog owners must be certain they are quite clear about the principles of housetraining *before* they get a dog. Early misbehaviors quickly become established as the *status quo*—becoming firmly entrenched as hard-to-break bad habits, which set the precedent for years to come. Make sure to teach your dog good habits right from the start. Good habits are just as hard to break as bad ones!

Ideally, when a new dog comes home, try to arrange for someone to be present as much as possible

HOUSETRAINING 1-2-3

1. Prevent Mistakes. When you can't supervise your puppy, confine her in a single room or in her crate (but don't leave her for too long!). Puppy-proof the area by laying down newspapers so that if she does make a mistake, it won't matter.

2. Teach Where. Take your puppy to the spot you want her to use every hour.

3. When she goes, praise her profusely and give her three favorite treats.

during the first few days (for adult dogs) or weeks for puppies. With only a little forethought, it is surprisingly easy to find a puppy sitter, such as a retired person, who would be willing to eat from your refrigerator and watch your television while keeping an eye on the newcomer to encourage the dog to play with chew toys and to ensure she goes outside on a regular basis.

Potty Training

Follow these steps to teach the dog where she should relieve herself:

1. never let her make a single mistake;

2. let her know where you want her to go; and

3. handsomely reward her for doing so: "GOOOOOOOD DOG!!!" liver treat, liver treat, liver treat!

Preventing Mistakes

A single mistake is a training disaster, since it heralds many more in future weeks. And each time the dog soils the house, this further reinforces the dog's unfortunate preference for an indoor, carpeted toilet. Do not let an unhousetrained dog have full run of the house.

When you are away from home, or cannot pay full attention, confine the dog to an area where elimination is appropriate, such as an outdoor run or, better still, a small, comfortable indoor kennel with access to an outdoor run. When confined in this manner, most dogs will naturally housetrain themselves.

If that's not possible, confine the dog to an area, such as a utility room, kitchen, basement or garage, where elimination may not be desired in the long run but as an interim measure it is certainly preferable to doing it all around the house. Use newspaper to cover the floor of the dog's day room. The

newspaper may be used to soak up the urine and to wrap up and dispose of the feces. Once your dog develops a preferred spot for eliminating, it is only necessary to cover that part of the floor with newspaper. The smaller papered area may then be moved (only a little each day) towards the door to the outside. Thus the dog will develop the tendency to go to the door when she needs to relieve herself.

Never confine an unhousetrained dog to a crate for long periods. Doing so would force the dog to soil the crate and ruin its usefulness as an aid for housetraining (see the following discussion).

Teaching Where

In order to teach your dog where you would like her to do her business, you have to be there to direct the proceedings—an obvious, yet often neglected, fact of life. In order to be there to teach the dog where to go, you need to know *when* she needs to go. Indeed, the success of housetraining depends on the owner's ability to predict these times. Certainly, a regular feeding schedule will facilitate prediction somewhat, but there is nothing like "loading the deck" and influencing the timing of the outcome yourself!

Whenever you are at home, make sure the dog is under constant supervision and/or confined to a small area. If already well trained, simply instruct the dog to lie down in her bed or basket. Alternatively, confine the dog to a crate (doggy den) or tie-down (a short, 18-inch lead that can be clipped to an eye hook in the baseboard near her bed). Short-term close confinement strongly inhibits urination and defecation, since the dog does not want to soil her sleeping area. Thus, when you release the puppydog each hour, she will definitely need to urinate immediately and defecate every third or fourth hour. Keep the dog confined to her doggy den and take her to her intended toilet area each hour, every hour and on the hour. When taking your dog outside, instruct her to sit quietly before opening the door—she will soon learn to sit by the door when she needs to go out!

Teaching Why

Being able to predict when the dog needs to go enables the owner to be on the spot to praise and reward the dog. Each hour, hurry the dog to the intended toilet area in the yard, issue the appropriate instruction ("Go pee!" or "Go poop!"), then give the dog three to four minutes to produce. Praise and offer a couple of training treats when successful. The treats are important because many people fail to praise their dogs with feeling . . . and housetraining is hardly the time for understatement. So either loosen up and enthusiastically praise that dog: "Wuzzzerwuzzer-wuzzer, hoooser good wuffer den? Hoooo went pee for Daddy?" Or say "Good dog!" as best you can and offer the treats for effect.

Following elimination is an ideal time for a spot of play-training in the yard or house. Also, an empty dog may be allowed greater freedom around the house for the next half hour or so, just as long as you keep an eye out to make sure she does not get into other kinds of mischief. If you are preoccupied and cannot pay full attention, confine the dog to her doggy den once more to enjoy a peaceful snooze or to play with her many chew toys.

If your dog does not eliminate within the allotted time outside—no biggie! Back to her doggy den, and then try again after another hour.

As I own large dogs, I always feel more relaxed walking an empty dog, knowing that I will not need to finish our stroll weighted down with bags of feces!

Beware of falling into the trap of walking the dog to get her to eliminate. The good ol' dog walk is such an enormous highlight in the dog's life that it represents the single biggest potential reward in domestic dogdom. However, when in a hurry, or during inclement weather, many owners abruptly terminate the walk the moment the dog has done her business. This, in effect, severely punishes the dog for doing the right thing, in the right place at the right time. Consequently, many dogs become strongly inhibited from eliminating outdoors because they know it will signal an abrupt end to an otherwise thoroughly enjoyable walk.

Instead, instruct the dog to relieve herself in the yard prior to going for a walk. If you follow the above instructions, most dogs soon learn to eliminate on cue. As soon as the dog eliminates, praise (and offer a treat or two)—"Good dog! Let's go walkies!" Use the walk as a reward for eliminating in the yard. If the dog does not go, put her back in

her doggy den and think about a walk later on. You will find with a "No feces—no walk" policy, your dog will become one of the fastest defecators in the business.

If you do not have a backyard, instruct the dog to eliminate right outside your front door prior to the walk. Not only will this facilitate clean up and disposal of the feces in your own trash can but, also, the walk may again be used as a colossal reward.

CHEWING AND BARKING

Short-term close confinement also teaches the dog that occasional quiet moments are a reality of domestic living. Your puppydog is extremely impressionable during her first few weeks at home. Regular confinement at this time soon exerts a calming influence over the dog's personality. Remember, once the dog is housetrained and calmer, there will be a whole lifetime ahead for the dog to enjoy full run of the house and garden. On the other hand, by letting the newcomer have unrestricted access to the entire household and allowing her to run willy-nilly, she will most certainly develop a bunch of behavior problems in short order, no doubt necessitating confinement later in life. It would not be fair to remedially restrain and confine a dog you have trained, through neglect, to run free.

When confining the dog, make sure she always has an impressive array of suitable chew toys. Kongs and sterilized longbones (both readily available from pet stores) make the best chew toys, since they are hollow and may be stuffed with treats to heighten the dog's interest. For example, by stuffing the little hole at the top of a Kong with a small piece of freeze-dried liver, the dog will not want to leave it alone.

Remember, treats do not have to be junk food and they certainly should not represent extra calories. Rather, treats should be part of each dog's regular daily diet: Some food may be served in the dog's bowl for breakfast and dinner, some food may be used as training treats, and some food may be used for stuffing chew toys. I regularly stuff my dogs' many Kongs with different shaped biscuits and kibble. The kibble seems to fall out fairly easily, as do the oval-shaped biscuits, thus rewarding the dog instantaneously for checking out the chew toys. The bone-shaped biscuits fall out after a while, rewarding the dog for worrying at the chew toy. But the triangular biscuits never come out. They remain inside the Kong as lures, maintaining the dog's fascination with her chew toy. To further focus the dog's interest, I always make sure to flavor the triangular biscuits by rubbing them with a little cheese or freeze-dried liver.

If stuffed chew toys are reserved especially for times the dog is confined, the puppydog will soon learn to enjoy quiet moments in her doggy den and she will quickly develop a chew-toy habit—a good habit! This is a simple autoshaping process; all the owner has to do is set up the situation and the dog all but trains herself—easy and effective. Even when the dog is given run of the house, her first inclination will be to indulge her rewarding chew-toy habit rather than destroy less-attractive household articles, such as curtains, carpets, chairs and compact disks. Similarly, a chew-toy chewer will be less inclined to scratch and chew herself excessively. Also, if the dog busies herself as a recreational chewer, she will be less inclined to develop into a recreational barker or digger when left at home alone.

Introducing your puppy to the chew toy will keep her from chewing up your shoes, and it will certainly remain your pet's favorite hobby into her adult years.

Stuff a number of chew toys whenever the dog is left confined and remove the extra-special-tasting treats when you return. Your dog will now amuse herself with her chew toys before falling asleep and then resume playing with her chew toys when she expects you to return. Since most owner-absent misbehavior happens right after you leave and right before your expected return, your puppydog will now be conveniently preoccupied with her chew toys at these times.

COME AND SIT

Most puppies will happily approach virtually anyone, whether called or not; that is, until they collide with adolescence and develop other more important doggy interests, such as sniffing a multiplicity of exquisite odors on the grass. Your mission, Mr./Ms. Owner, is to teach and reward the pup for coming reliably, willingly and happily when called—and you have just three months to get it done. Unless adequately reinforced, your puppy's tendency to approach people will self-destruct by adolescence.

Call your dog ("Fido, come!"), open your arms (and maybe squat down) as a welcoming signal, waggle a treat or toy as a lure and reward the puppydog when she comes running. Do not wait to praise the dog until she reaches you—she may come 95 percent of the way and then run off after some distraction. Instead, praise the dog's first step towards you and continue praising enthusiastically for every step she takes in your direction.

When the rapidly approaching puppy dog is three lengths away from impact, instruct her to sit ("Fido, sit!") and hold the lure in front of you in an outstretched hand to prevent her from hitting you mid-chest and knocking you flat on your back! As Fido decelerates to nose the lure, move the treat upwards and backwards just over her muzzle with an upwards motion of your extended arm (palm-upwards). As the dog looks up to follow the lure, she will sit down (if she jumps up, you are holding the lure too high). Praise the dog for sitting. Move backwards and call her again. Repeat this many times over, always praising when Fido comes and sits; on occasion, reward her.

For the first couple of trials, use a training treat both as a lure to entice the dog to come and sit and as a reward for doing so. Thereafter, try to use different items as lures and rewards. For example, lure the dog with a Kong or Frisbee but reward her with a food treat. Or lure the dog with a food treat but pat her and throw a tennis ball as a reward. After just a few repetitions, dispense with the lures and rewards; the dog will begin to respond willingly to your verbal requests and hand signals just for the prospect of praise from your heart and affection from your hands.

Instruct every family member, friend and visitor how to get the dog to come and sit. Invite people over for a series of pooch parties; do not keep the pup a secret—let other people enjoy this puppy, and let the pup enjoy other people. Puppydog parties are not only fun, they easily attract a lot of people to help you train your dog. Unless you teach your dog how to meet people, that is, to sit for greetings, no doubt the dog will resort to jumping up. Then you and the visitors will get annoyed, and the dog will be punished. This is not fair. Send out those invitations for puppy parties and teach your dog to be mannerly and socially acceptable.

Even though your dog quickly masters obedient recalls in the house, her reliability may falter when playing in the backyard or local park. Ironically, it is the owner who has unintentionally trained the dog not to respond in these

This woman is praising her Pom for walking nicely outside on leash.

especially fast recalls, offer a couple of training treats and take the time to praise and pet the dog enthusiastically before releasing her. The dog will learn that coming when called is not necessarily the end of the play session, and neither is it the end of the world; rather, it signals an enjoyable, quality time-out with the owner before resuming play once more. In fact, playing in the park now becomes a very effective life-reward, which works to facilitate training by reinforcing each obedient and timely recall. Good news!

SIT, DOWN, STAND AND ROLLOVER

Teaching the dog a variety of body positions is easy for owner and dog, impressive for spectators and extremely useful for all. Using lure-reward techniques, it is possible to train several positions at once to verbal commands or hand signals (which impress the socks off onlookers).

Sit and down—the two control commands—prevent or resolve nearly a hundred behavior problems. For example, if the dog happily and obediently sits or lies down when requested, she cannot jump on

instances. By allowing the dog to play and run around and otherwise have a good time, but then to call the dog to put her on leash to take her home, the dog quickly learns playing is fun but training is a drag. Thus, playing in the park becomes a severe distraction, which works against training. Bad news!

Instead, whether playing with the dog off leash or on leash, request her to come at frequent intervals—say, every minute or so. On most occasions, praise and pet the dog for a few seconds while she is sitting, then tell her to go play again. For visitors, dash out the front door, run around and chase her tail, pester other dogs, harass cats or annoy family, friends or strangers. Additionally, "Sit" or "Down" are the best emergency commands for off-leash control.

It is easier to teach and maintain a reliable sit than maintain a reliable recall. Sit is the purest and simplest of commands—either the dog is sitting or she is not. If there is any change of circumstances or potential danger in the park, for example, simply instruct the dog to sit. If she sits, you have a number of options: Allow the dog to resume playing when she is safe, walk up and put the dog on leash or call the dog. The dog will be much more likely to come when called if she has already acknowledged her compliance by sitting. If the dog does not sit in the park—train her to!

Stand and rollover-stay are the two positions for examining the dog. Your veterinarian will love you to distraction if you take a little time to teach the dog to stand still and roll over and play possum. Also, your vet bills will be smaller because it will take the veterinarian less time to examine your dog. The rollover-stay is an especially useful command and

is really just a variation of the down-stay: Whereas the dog lies prone in the traditional down, she lies supine in the rollover-stay.

As with teaching come and sit, the training techniques to teach the dog to assume all other body positions on cue are user-friendly and dog-friendly. Simply give the appropriate request, lure the dog into the desired body position using a training treat or toy and then praise (and maybe reward) the dog as soon as she complies. Try not to touch the dog to get her to respond. If you teach the dog by guiding her into position, the dog will quickly learn that rump-pressure means sit, for

This Pom complies with her owner's "sit" command.

example, but as yet you still have no control over your dog if she is just 6 feet away. It will still be necessary to teach the dog to sit on request. So do not make training a time-consuming two-step process; instead, teach the dog to sit to a verbal request or hand signal from the outset. Once the dog sits willingly when requested, by all means use your hands to pet the dog when she does so.

To teach down when the dog is already sitting, say "Fido, down!", hold the lure in one hand (palm down) and lower that hand to the floor between the dog's forepaws. As

Communicating with your Pom by talking to her and offering treats will make training more effective and fun for the both of you!

the dog lowers her head to follow the lure, slowly move the lure away from the dog just a fraction (in front of her paws). The dog will lie down as she stretches her nose forward to follow the lure. Praise the dog when she does so. If the dog stands up, you pulled the lure away too far and too quickly.

When teaching the dog to lie down from the standing position, say "Down" and lower the lure to the floor as before. Once the dog has lowered her forequarters and assumed a play bow, gently and slowly move the lure towards the dog between her forelegs. Praise the dog as soon as her rear end plops down.

After just a couple of trials it will be possible to alternate sits and downs and have the dog energetically perform doggy push-ups. Praise the dog a lot, and after half a dozen or so push-ups reward the dog with a training treat or toy. You will notice the more energetically you move your arm—upwards (palm up) to get the dog to sit, and downwards (palm down) to get the dog to lie down—the more energetically the dog responds to your requests. Now try training the dog in silence and you will notice she has also learned to respond to hand signals. Yeah! Not too shabby for the first session.

To teach stand from the sitting position, say "Fido, stand," slowly move the lure half a dog-length away from the dog's nose, keeping it at nose level, and praise the dog as she stands to follow the lure. As soon as the dog stands, lower the lure to just beneath the dog's chin to entice her to look down; otherwise she will stand and then sit immediately. To prompt the dog to stand from the down position, move the lure half a dog-length upwards and away from the dog, holding the lure at standing nose height from the floor.

Teaching rollover is best started from the down position, with the dog lying on one side, or at least with both hind legs stretched out on the same side. Say "Fido, bang!" and move the lure backwards and alongside the dog's muzzle to her elbow (on the side of her outstretched hind legs). Once the dog looks to the side and backwards, very slowly move the lure upwards to the dog's shoulder and backbone. Tickling the dog in the goolies (groin area) often invokes a reflex-raising of the hind leg as an appeasement gesture, which facilitates the tendency to roll over. If you move the lure too

FINDING A TRAINER

Have fun with your dog, take a training class! But don't just sign on any dotted line, find a trainer whose approach and style you like and whose students (and their dogs) are really learning. Ask to visit a class to observe a trainer in action. For the names of trainers near you, ask your veterinarian, your pet supply store, your dog-owning neighbors or call (800) PET-DOGS (the Association of Pet Dog Trainers.)

quickly and the dog jumps into the standing position, have patience and start again. As soon as the dog rolls onto her back, keep the lure stationary and mesmerize the dog with a relaxing tummy rub.

To teach rollover-stay when the dog is standing or moving, say "Fido, bang!" and give the appropriate hand signal (with index finger pointed and thumb cocked in true Sam Spade fashion), then in one fluid movement lure her to first lie down and then rollover-stay as above.

Teaching the dog to stay in each of the above four positions becomes a piece of cake after first teaching the dog not to worry at the toy or treat training lure. This is best accomplished by hand feeding dinner kibble. Hold a piece of kibble

TOYS THAT EARN THEIR KEEP

To entertain even the most distracted of dogs, while you're home or away, have a selection of the following toys on hand: hollow chew toys (like Kongs, sterilized hollow longbones and cubes or balls that can be stuffed with kibble). Smear peanut butter or honey on the inside of the hollow toy or bone, stuff the bone with kibble and your dog will think of nothing else but working the object to get at the food. Great to take your dog's mind off the fact that you've left the house.

82

firmly in your hand and softly instruct "Off!" Ignore any licking and slobbering for however long the dog worries at the treat, but say "Take it!" and offer the kibble the instant the dog breaks contact with her muzzle. Repeat this a few times, and then up the ante and insist the dog remove her muzzle for one whole second before offering the kibble. Then progressively refine your criteria and have the dog not touch your hand (or treat) for longer and longer periods on each trial, such as for two seconds, four seconds, then six, ten, fifteen, twenty, thirty seconds and so on.

The dog soon learns: (1) worrying at the treat never gets results, whereas (2) noncontact is often rewarded after a variable time lapse.

Teaching "Off!" has many useful applications in its own right. Additionally, instructing the dog not to touch a training lure often produces spontaneous and magical stays. Request the dog to stand-stay, for example, and not to touch the lure. At first set your sights on a short two-second stay before rewarding the dog. (Remember, every long journey begins with a single step.) However, on subsequent trials, gradually and progressively increase the length of stay required to receive a reward. In no time at all your dog will stand calmly for a minute or so.

RELEVANCY TRAINING

Once you have taught the dog what you expect her to do when requested to come, sit, lie down, stand, rollover and stay, the time is right to teach the dog why she should comply with your wishes. The secret is to have many (many) extremely short training interludes (two to five seconds each) at numerous (numerous) times during the course of the dog's day. Especially work with the dog immediately before the dog's good times and during the dog's good times. For example, ask your dog to sit and/or lie down each time before opening doors, serving meals, offering treats and tummy rubs; ask the dog to perform a few controlled doggy push-ups before letting her off leash or throwing a tennis ball; and perhaps request the dog to sit-down-sit-stand-down-stand-rollover before inviting her to cuddle on the couch.

Similarly, request the dog to sit many times during play or on walks, and in no time at all the dog will be only too pleased to follow your instructions because she has learned that a compliant response heralds all sorts of goodies. Basically all you are trying to teach the dog is how to say please: "Please throw the tennis ball. Please may I snuggle on the couch."

Remember, it is important to keep training interludes short and to have many short sessions each and every day. The shortest (and most useful) session comprises asking the dog to sit and then go play during a play session. When trained this way, your dog will soon associate training with good times. In fact, the dog may be unable to distinguish between training and good times and, indeed, there should be no

distinction. The warped concept that training involves forcing the dog to comply and/or dominating her will is totally at odds with the picture of a truly well-trained dog. In reality, enjoying a game of training with a dog is no different from enjoying a game of backgammon or tennis with a friend; and walking with a dog should be no different from strolling with a spouse, or with buddies on the golf course.

FOLLOWING

Start by training your dog to follow you. Many puppies will follow if you simply walk away from them and maybe click your fingers or chuckle. Adult dogs may require additional enticement to stimulate them to follow, such as a training lure or, at the very least, a lively trainer. To teach the dog to follow: (1) keep walking and (2) walk away from the dog. If the dog attempts to lead or lag, change pace; slow down if the dog forges too far ahead, but speed up if she lags too far behind. Say "Steady!" or "Easy!" each time before you slow down and "Quickly!" or "Hustle!" each time before you speed up, and the dog will learn to change pace on cue. If the dog lags or leads too far, or if she wanders right or left, simply walk quickly in the opposite direction and maybe even run away from the dog and hide.

Practicing is a lot of fun; you can set up a course in your home, yard or park to do this. Indoors, entice the dog to follow upstairs, into a bedroom, into the bathroom, downstairs, around the living room couch, zigzagging between dining room chairs and into the kitchen for dinner. Outdoors, get the dog to follow around park benches, trees, shrubs and along walkways and lines in the grass. (For safety outdoors, it is advisable to attach a long line on the dog, but never exert corrective tension on the line.)

Remember, following has a lot to do with attitude—your attitude! Most probably your dog will not want to follow Mr. Grumpy Troll with the personality of wilted lettuce. Lighten up—walk with a jaunty step, whistle a happy tune, sing, skip and tell jokes to your dog and she will be right there by your side.

No Pulling on Leash

You can start teaching your dog not to pull on leash anywhere—in front of the television or outdoors—but regardless of location, you must not take a single step with tension in the leash. For a reason known only to dogs, even just a couple of paces of pulling on leash is intrinsically motivating and diabolically rewarding. Instead, attach the leash to the dog's collar, grasp the other end firmly with both hands held close to your chest, and stand still—do not budge an inch. Have somebody watch you with a stopwatch to time your progress, or else you will never believe this will work and so you will not even try the exercise, and your shoulder and the dog's neck will be traumatized for years to come.

Stand still and wait for the dog to stop pulling, and to sit and/or lie down. All dogs stop pulling and sit eventually. Most take only a couple of minutes; the all-time record is $22\frac{1}{2}$ minutes. Time how long it takes. Gently praise the dog when she stops pulling, and as soon as she sits, enthusiastically praise the dog and take just one step forward, then immediately stand still. This single step usually demonstrates the ballistic reinforcing nature of pulling on leash; most dogs explode to the end of the leash, so be prepared for the strain. Stand firm and wait for the

This owner is proud to walk with her calm, well-trained dog.

dog to sit again. Repeat this half a dozen times and you will probably notice a progressive reduction in the force of the dog's one-step explosions and a radical reduction in the time it takes for the dog to sit each time.

As the dog learns "Sit we go" and "Pull we stop," she will begin to walk forward calmly with each single step and automatically sit when you stop. Now try two steps before you stop. Wooooooo! Scary! When the dog has mastered two steps at a time, try for three. After each success, progressively increase the number of steps in the sequence: try four steps and then six, eight, ten and twenty steps before stopping. Congratulations! You are now walking the dog on leash.

Whenever walking with the dog (off leash or on leash), make sure you stop periodically to practice a few position commands and stays before instructing the dog to "Walk on!"

Integrating training into a walk offers 200 separate opportunities to use the continuance of the walk as a reward to reinforce the dog's education.

CHAPTER NINE

Resources

BOOKS

About Pomeranians

Hughes, Pauline B. *The Pomeranian.* Fairfax, VA: Denlingers Pub Ltd., 1990.

Tietjen, Sari Brewster. *The New Pomeranian.* New York: Howell Book House, 1987.

About Health Care

American Kennel Club. *American Kennel Club Dog Care and Training.* New York: Howell Book House, 1991.

Carlson, Delbert, DVM, and James Giffen, MD. *Dog Owner's Home Veterinary Handbook.* New York: Howell Book House, 1992.

DeBitetto, James, DVM, and Sarah Hodgson. *You & Your Puppy.* New York: Howell Book House, 1995.

Lane, Marion. *The Humane Society of the United States Complete Guide to Dog Care.* New York: Little, Brown & Co., 1998.

McGinnis, Terri. *The Well Dog Book.* New York: Random House, 1991.

Schwartz, Stephanie, DVM. *First Aid for Dogs: An Owner's Guide to a Happy Healthy Pet.* New York: Howell Book House, 1998.

Volhard, Wendy and Kerry L. Brown. *The Holistic Guide for a Healthy Dog.* New York: Howell Book House, 1995.

About Training

Ammen, Amy. *Training in No Time.* New York: Howell Book House, 1995.

Benjamin, Carol Lea. *Mother Knows Best.* New York: Howell Book House, 1985.

Bohnenkamp, Gwen. *Manners for the Modern Dog.* San Francisco: Perfect Paws, 1990.

Dunbar, Ian, Ph.D., MRCVS. *Dr. Dunbar's Good Little Book.* James & Kenneth Publishers, 2140 Shattuck Ave. #2406, Berkeley, CA 94704. (510) 658-8588. Order from Publisher.

Evans, Job Michael. *People, Pooches and Problems.* New York: Howell Book House, 1991.

Palika, Liz. *All Dogs Need Some Training.* New York: Howell Book House, 1997.

Volhard, Jack and Melissa Bartlett. *What All Good Dogs Should Know: The Sensible Way to Train.* New York: Howell Book House, 1991.

About Activities

Hall, Lynn. *Dog Showing for Beginners.* New York: Howell Book House, 1994.

O'Neil, Jackie. *All About Agility.* New York: Howell Book House, 1998.

Simmons-Moake, Jane. *Agility Training, The Fun Sport for All Dogs.* New York: Howell Book House, 1991.

Vanacore, Connie. *Dog Showing: An Owner's Guide.* New York: Howell Book House, 1990.

Volhard, Jack and Wendy. *The Canine Good Citizen.* New York: Howell Book House, 1994.

MAGAZINES

The AKC GAZETTE, The Official Journal for the Sport of Purebred Dogs
American Kennel Club
260 Madison Ave.
New York, NY 10016
www.akc.org

Dog Fancy
Fancy Publications
3 Burroughs
Irvine, CA 92618
(714) 855-8822
http://dogfancy.com

Dog & Kennel
7-L Dundas Circle
Greensboro, NC 27407
(336) 292-4047
www.dogandkennel.com

Dog World
Maclean Hunter Publishing Corp.
500 N. Dearborn, Ste. 1100
Chicago, IL 60610
(312) 396-0600
www.dogworldmag.com

PetLife: Your Companion Animal Magazine
Magnolia Media Group
1400 Two Tandy Center
Fort Worth, TX 76102
(800) 767-9377
www.petlifeweb.com

MORE INFORMATION ABOUT POMERANIANS

National Breed Club

AMERICAN POMERANIAN CLUB, INC.
Corresponding Secretary:
  Brenda Turner
  3910 Concord Place
  Texarkana, TX 75501-2212

Breeder Contact:
  Jane Lehtinen
  1325 9th St., S.
  Virginia, MN 55792
  (218) 741-5336

Breed Rescue:
  Linda Brogoitti
  (602) 979-5336

The Club can send you information on all aspects of the breed including the names and addresses of breed clubs in your area, as well as obedience clubs. Inquire about membership.

The American Kennel Club

The American Kennel Club (AKC), devoted to the advancement of purebred dogs, is the oldest and largest registry organization in this country. Every breed recognized by the AKC has a national (parent) club. National clubs are a great source of information on your breed. The affiliated clubs hold AKC events and use AKC rules to hold performance events, dog shows, educational programs, health clinics and training classes. The AKC staff is divided between offices in New York City and Raleigh, North Carolina. The AKC has an excellent Web site that provides information on the organization and all AKC-recognized breeds. The address is www.akc.org.

For registration and performance events information, or for customer service, contact:

THE AMERICAN KENNEL CLUB
5580 Centerview Dr., Suite 200
Raleigh, NC 27606
(919) 233-9767

The AKC's executive offices and the AKC Library (open to the public) are at this address:

THE AMERICAN KENNEL CLUB
260 Madison Ave.
New York, New York 10016
(212) 696-8200 (general information)
(212) 696-8246 (AKC Library)
www.akc.org

UNITED KENNEL CLUB
100 E. Kilgore Rd.
Kalamazoo, MI 49001-5598
(616) 343-9020
www.ukcdogs.com

AMERICAN RARE BREED ASSOCIATION
9921 Frank Tippett Rd.
Cheltenham, MD 20623
(301) 868-5718 (voice or fax)
www.arba.org

CANADIAN KENNEL CLUB
89 Skyway Ave., Ste. 100
Etobicoke, Ontario
Canada M9W 6R4
(416) 675-5511
www.ckc.ca

ORTHOPEDIC FOUNDATION FOR ANIMALS (OFA)
2300 E. Nifong Blvd.
Columbia, MO 65201-3856
(314) 442-0418
www.offa.org

Trainers

Animal Behavior & Training Associates (ABTA)
9018 Balboa Blvd., Ste. 591
Northridge, CA 91325
(800) 795-3294
www.Good-dawg.com

Association of Pet Dog Trainers
(APDT)
(800) PET-DOGS
www.apdt.com

National Association of Dog Obedience
Instructors (NADOI)
729 Grapevine Highway, Ste. 369
Hurst, TX 76054-2085
www.kimberly.uidaho.edu/nadoi

Associations

Delta Society
P.O. Box 1080
Renton, WA 98507-1080
(Promotes the human/animal bond
through pet-assisted therapy and other
programs)
www.petsforum.com/
DELTASOCIETY/dsi400.htm

Dog Writers Association of America
(DWAA)
Pat Santi, Secretary
222 Woodchuck Lane
Harwinton, CT 06791
www.dwaa.org

National Association for Search and
Rescue (NASAR)
4500 Southgate Place, Ste. 100
Chantilly, VA 20157
(703) 222-6277
www.nasar.org

Therapy Dogs International
6 Hilltop Rd.
Mendham, NJ 07945

OTHER USEFUL RESOURCES—WEB SITES

General Information— Links to Additional Sites, On-Line Shopping

www.k9web.com –resources for the dog world

www.netpet.com – pet related products, software and services

www.apapets.com – The American Pet Association

www.dogandcatbooks.com – a complete selection of dog and cat books

www.dogbooks.com – on-line bookshop

www.animal.discovery.com/ – cable television channel on-line

Health

www.avma.org – American Veterinary Medical Association (AVMA)

www.aplb.org – Association for Pet Loss Bereavement (APLB)—contains an index of national hot lines for on-line and office counseling.

www.netfopets.com/AskTheExperts.html – veterinary questions answered on-line.

Breed Information

www.bestdogs.com/news/ – newsgroup

www.cheta.net/connect/canine/breeds/ – Canine Connections Breed Information Index

89